HOW TO MANAGE YOUR MONEY LIKE AN ADULT IN 7 EASY STEPS

SAVE MONEY, CREATE AND STICK TO A BUDGET, STOP
LIVING PAYCHECK TO PAYCHECK, AND FIND
FINANCIAL INDEPENDENCE

MORGAN JOHNS

D1714183

ACKNOWLEDGMENTS

I am very grateful to be able to share this information with you but I have not done this alone. I would firstly like to thank my parents, who put their faith in me and instilled confidence in my decision making from an early age. I would also like to thank my partner who has provided unwavering support with all my endeavors but also made me accountable to realize my end goals. To my brother who challenges me but has encouraged me during critical times when I doubted myself.

It's a fair statement to say that the finance, property and investment sector can attract an array of characters and it was important to me to work with people and businesses, whose values and ethics aligned with my own and where the client always came first. I am very lucky to have worked for the best, where the standard was set high, where I can honestly say that our clients lives changed (financially) for the better and have met colleagues and associates who have become lifelong friends along the way.

Lastly to my children. They are my inspiration which instilled the desire to be better and do better.

CONTENTS

To become financially independent, you must turn part of your income into capital; turn capital into enterprise; turn enterprise into profit; turn profit into investment; and turn investment into financial independence. –Jim Rohn

INTRODUCTION

"It's okay, you are just a child. You are allowed to make mistakes."

I was consoling my 10-year-old niece who had spent all her pocket money on something stupid. She had received the money a couple of days back, and within this time she spent all of it. Now she had no money left. As I was trying to calm her down, I had the most shocking revelation: Most of us often do the same thing. The day we get paid, we spend lavishly on things that we don't need and regret it the next day. There have even been weeks when we had to cut back on something essential because we made a silly purchase. How does that make us different from the 10-year-old? Are we not supposed to be the 'adults' here?

It got me thinking, many of us can be surprisingly immature when it comes to money. Just the other day, my 35-year-old neighbor spent a ridiculous amount on a PlayStation. He says he bought it for his kid, but his wife told me the real truth—ever since the PlayStation has come, it's like he has forgotten his life and wife! That's not the kind of behavior you would expect from a man at that age, is it?

Let us look at another scenario. Kathryn is a 45-year-old

married woman with two teenagers. Both Kathryn and her husband work, but she often feels like they are not saving enough. The children are now in school, and her daughter Heather aspires to go to medical school. While that is a matter of immense pride for the parents, Kathryn is not sure if they will be able to afford it. Moreover, no matter how hard she tries to teach her kids to be judicious and spend carefully, they spend lavishly on things they don't even use after a while—last month Heather bought a pair of boots for $75 and now they make her feet hurt.

Deep in her heart, Kathryn knows that her children got this habit from her. She often splurges on things that she can't afford, only to feel guilty and struggle financially later on. The other day, she went to the supermarket to buy groceries. The snacks counter is always tempting and that day she ended up buying packs of chips, candy bars, and marshmallows. Kathryn justified the purchases by telling herself, *We need snacks during our weekly movie nights. It's okay, it's not much.* If I was being honest with you, Kathryn had bought so many snacks that she could feed the entire neighborhood during a movie night.

The guilt from buying so much unhealthy food was eating Kathryn up. She had to do something about it. So she went to the healthy foods section and bought a ton of quinoa, rolled oats, organic vegetables, and meat. She even made a mental note of all the healthy detox recipes she saw on Instagram. As she was heading to the checkout counter, she saw a sale on avocados. Kathryn's husband loved avocado toast, so she thought she could make it for breakfast the next day. She ended up buying a dozen of them. Anyone with a sane mind knows that avocados go bad quickly and it is impossible to eat that many in such a short time. The urge to buy something whenever she sees the word 'sale' made Kathryn waste her money on something she won't be able to use.

When the shopping was done and the cashier handed her the

bill, Kathryn's heart sank. She had spent too much. For the next few days, she was going to have to mind every dollar that she spent. As she paid the bill and walked out of the store, she was filled with anger and disappointment. Even after working for so many years, she had to think before buying some extra groceries. When a supermarket bill could make her feel poor, what was her financial condition? What was she doing with her life?

The situations might have been different but we have all felt the way Kathryn did at some point in our lives. Not many people are completely satisfied with their financial situation (except for multi-millionaires maybe?) and we are always searching for ways to improve it. However, in most cases, these efforts go in vain because nobody knows how to manage their money properly. Even people with finance degrees struggle with simple things like budgeting and saving enough. Everyone is happy when the money starts coming in, but nobody will tell you how to manage it. This is something that you are expected to know. But when you can't manage, things get out of control and you blame yourself for not being good with your money. If you have felt like this, then you are not alone. Don't beat yourself up for not being good at financial management because most people are not.

Circling back to where I started, I want to emphasize that children and adults both make mistakes with money. However, society is much harder on adults because they are always expected to make the right decision. I want us to break this chain of thought together. You can be an adult and make mistakes because it is not easy to get everything right on the first try. Whenever you are faced with a tempting choice, your heart wants to indulge in it. This is the moment when you have to stop and think about the situation. This is your opportunity to make a major change in your life. Most people have no idea how to manage money—and why would we? It's not like all of us have a Masters in finance or attended schools that had well-defined courses on money management. However, despite this ignorant attitude from our educational institutions, it is not okay to sit back and do nothing about it. The biggest blessing of being alive in the 21st century is that resources are easily available and you can do anything if you set your mind to it. In my many years of experience, I have seen people grow and develop good financial habits by making simple changes in their life. Everybody is capable of change, you just have to believe in yourself and make the decision to be disciplined and set systems in place. It's not that difficult but it takes some work. I understand your pain if you are feeling anxious about not having enough money. I have been in that situation and I made a promise to myself that I would not be passive and feel sorry for myself, that I would do something about it.

In this book, you will get comprehensive guidance on how to manage your money and stay on top of your financial goals in seven simple steps. We will analyze one problem at a time and solve them all so that you feel more confident with money. From budgeting to investing along with dilemmas about homeowner-ship, all your confusion will be clarified as you embark on this journey with me.

I firmly believe the reason why people don't like reading books on personal finance is that they feel like they are being lectured. I never liked lecturing or being lectured, which is why I want this to be a conversation between you and me. We will go through every problem together so that you can analyze what went wrong and how to improve. There will be exercises and special notes so that you know what to do if you are stuck. The purpose of the work-sheets is to create a space for you to actively 'do' something that will start nudging you along the way.

Taking Action

Before we start, I want to highlight the importance of taking action and being proactive about your financial future. The cost of doing nothing could result in living paycheck to paycheck, not having enough to retire on and suffering financial hardship. Personal finance is a wide umbrella, and it differs for everyone. Staying generic will get us nowhere and I want you to reach your goals after you are done with this book.

Now let's get personal and solve those money problems which have been bothering you for so long. The hardest part of solving a problem is getting started. Once the ball gets rolling, the problems become easier. You have already taken the first step and that makes you a champion.

So, without further ado, let's start the journey to financial independence. Cheers!

WHY SOCIETY SETS YOU UP TO
BE A FAILURE WITH MONEY

Too many people spend money they earned to buy things they don't want, to impress people they don't like. –Will Rogers

After a long, tiring week, it's finally Friday. It's around 3:00 p.m. and you get a text from your friends about a plan to meet in the evening. You have been looking forward to the weekend because you needed some time to unwind. So, you agree and head straight to the pub after you finish work. When your friends arrive, the drinking saga begins, and you start having the typical Friday fun. The drinks make you tipsy, and before you know it, you are flirting with the cute waiter. You don't remember any conversation because it's difficult to even remember your own name after four Margaritas!

The next morning, you wake up with a terrible hangover. When you check your phone, you are filled with regret, and it's not because of the waiter. You can't believe that you wasted so much money on drinks and dinner. You kept ordering the most expensive cocktails and then spent a fortune on food at that fancy restaurant.

All of your friends were doing it, so you went along and now you regret it. The drinks must have ignited all your stupid impulses because you know better than spending this much on food and drinks (or flirting with a waiter).

This happened many times in my twenties—I would get carried away in the moment, sometimes it's because I was busy keeping up with the Joneses (now the Kardashians), and sometimes it's a case of not wanting to be the killjoy or the person who is always too careful with their money.

I am not suggesting that you become a Scrooge and stop going out, but peer pressure often sets us up to do things that we would not have done otherwise. You know you want to be better with money but there are external forces at work that actively encourage the development of poor money management. Once you know the psychology behind this, you might be able to deal with it better.

HOW YOU ARE BECOMING A VICTIM OF FINANCIAL ILLITERACY

Let's go back to our high school days. Remember the classes that you had? English, French or Spanish, Math, History, Geography, Gym, and so on. Can you recall having any subject that was remotely related to financial management? You might have had the occasional seminar where someone from a bank would explain how banking operations worked, but many schools don't bother with such proactive measures. Maybe you learned about compound interest as a part of your arithmetic curriculum in any grade. Do you think that knowledge was sufficient for you to understand how it works? Compounding is one of the most important things to know in order to optimize your savings and investment strategy. Yet, you know so little about how it works.

Here is a frightening statistic, four in ten adults would not be able to pay a surprise bill of $400 from their funds and would have to sell any asset or borrow from someone (Board of Governors of the Federal Reserve System, 2018). This means that four out of ten adults are not completely prepared in case of a medical emergency or any other situation that requires urgent financial intervention. Can you believe how scary that is?

You must be feeling guilt and anxiety boiling up inside you, but don't blame yourself. Many of us grew up with the belief that it was 'impolite' to talk about money. A survey conducted by T. Rowe Price (2017) revealed that 69% of parents have admitted that they were reluctant to bring up the topic of finances with their children. Children learn most of the things in the home and it takes a long time to unlearn those things because those beliefs become fundamental to our existence. Even if we hate it, those beliefs are a part of us. This means that most American children feel hesitant to talk about money. It is unfortunate, but we only remember the things that we are forced to remember. When a school makes it compulsory to learn something, there is no way but to learn it. Despite the system being problematic, you end up learning about the subjects that you wouldn't have learned about otherwise. That is how you understood how the volcano works, what adjectives are, and which wars Napoleon fought.

Since nobody formally teaches money management in school, young adults have no clue about some of the most important things when it comes to personal finance. They graduate and enter the real world without any knowledge of budgeting, saving, investing, or how to manage their debt. According to the New York Federal Reserve, consumer debt reached $14.56 trillion by the fourth quarter of 2020 (Fay, 2019). Despite these enormous debt figures, the country is filled with budding citizens who do not understand the basics of how to manage it.

One common thing among talented actors, athletes, and

speakers is that they are always prepared for the things that matter the most to them. You would not expect an Olympic gymnast to show up to a game without any training. For the average person, even though money management plays an essential role in determining their quality of life, most people step into the process thoroughly unprepared. This puts them in a tough spot and makes them vulnerable to making wrong financial decisions and racking up debts. These adults grow into parents who feel hesitant to talk about money with their kids and the cycle of financial illiteracy continues.

Since we are conditioned to think that whatever the majority is doing is correct, most of the time we fail to see the fundamentally problematic systems that we are a part of. It's easier to blame yourself. However, when you decode these practices, you will understand that your financial illiteracy had very little to do with you.

THE CURSE OF THE NUMEROUS PAYMENT OPTIONS

As you delve deeper into unraveling the mystery behind our systematic financial illiteracy, you will see how this ignorance makes us oblivious to certain things. Our previous generation was constantly thinking about things they could or could not afford, including the idea that if you did not earn enough then you could not afford a house, a nice car, or good clothes. Today, economic development has made it easy for everyone to afford everything. Credit cards and other installment-based payment facilities have made the buying process simpler and has created an illusion that you can afford practically anything. Let us look into these payment options and how they can mess up personal financial management.

Credit Cards

When you own a credit card, you can buy anything as permitted by the limit set on your card. You might be earning $1,500 per week but your credit limit can be much higher than that amount. This makes you eligible to purchase things that are way beyond your actual affordability. Here is a list of reasons why you should avoid using credit cards unless absolutely necessary:

- It encourages impulse buying: Imagine you are at the mall and you see a pair of shoes which you instantly love (but don't need). You check out the price and realize that you don't have the cash to pay for it. As you are going through your wallet, you find your credit card. The price tag is hurting you, but the credit card is tempting you to make the purchase. Most of the time, you give in to the temptation and buy those shoes.
- It confuses your budget: Credit cards are like that cake shop located outside your gym. After an intense workout, when you are feeling hungry, a cake is the last thing that you should have. But when you see the glorious cupcakes and cheesecakes on display, you simply cannot resist. You might have been maintaining a strict budget, but credit cards enable you to spend beyond your means. Once you start indulging yourself in it, budgeting becomes useless.
- You end up spending more: Credit cards are the highest interest-bearing consumer debt. You can end up incurring an interest rate as high as 20%, which means you might end up paying more than the actual expense. If you keep on paying the minimum amount every month, you will be paying interest on accumulated interest which can add up to a large amount very quickly.

The biggest issue that makes credit cards a supervillain in your journey toward money management is that you don't have to physically pay any cash upfront. You take out your card, tap or swipe it, and the payment is done. Since there is no physical outflow of cash, it keeps you in denial about how much you are spending and when you are going overboard. This is true for all such virtual modes of payment.

More than 191 million Americans use credit cards and the average household credit card debt is $5,315 (Fay, 2019). This is a surprising figure given that the average American adult does not have $400 for an emergency. Credit cards desensitize you to the reality of spending and increase your desire to purchase things. The desire to 'splurge' is enhanced when one is using a credit card.

Tap and Go Payments

These have become increasingly common after the Covid-19 pandemic hit the world. Contactless payments are very convenient because you just have to scan the QR code and make payments from your phone. This has been useful after the pandemic when the entire world is anxious to minimize contacts. It certainly has its uses but the damage that is being done is quite serious. The simplicity of contactless payments has made it difficult for us to feel accountable for how much we are spending. Contactless payments indulge the compulsive shopper because they do not have to pay cash.

Pay Later Options

"Buy Now, Pay Later" (BNPL) schemes are becoming increasingly popular among the younger generation. The providers of such schemes often team up with retailers to provide attractive offers to the customers. You can purchase something now and pay for the same at a later date. There will be no interest or late fees, which means the seller is giving you interest-free credit. It is very common for young people to use this facility for online shopping. This again enables them to own things that are beyond what they can afford. These schemes pose significant risks for both the borrower and lender. Since most borrowers conduct no background check before extending these credit facilities to a consumer, if the borrower defaults then the lender has to bear the risk, which is why most of these schemes are tied up with the borrower's credit card. If the borrower does not make the payment within the stipulated date, the amount will automatically be deducted from their credit card.

Installment payment systems have been there for ages, but it was mostly limited to high-value purchases like furniture, expensive electronic gadgets, etc. Buy now pay later schemes can be used to make smaller purchases and have gained more popularity in 2020 due to the pandemic. The average American's affordability fell to an all-time low because of the severe economic decline which is why BNPL schemes became convenient for online shopping.

If you have used such a scheme, you know they promise you interest-free repayments. However, if you read the terms and conditions carefully, you will find that there is a "late fee" in case you fail to repay the due on time. Credit cards can help you build good credit over time but BNPL schemes have no such benefit. Even if you make regular repayments, it won't affect your credit score and if you fail you have to incur high late fees and your credit gets hampered, which might be a problem when you are trying to buy a house, but more on that later.

Multiple payment options are supposed to make our lives easier. However, if we think about it, it actually does the exact opposite. Technology can often yield disastrous results if used incorrectly. I gifted an iPad to my Grandma last Christmas and although I set the device up properly, with all her contacts and even a few shopping apps in case she was ever out of essential items, curiosity got the best of her and she ended up downloading eBay. Before she could understand how to navigate the app, she tapped a few buttons and placed an order for an old Casablanca movie poster for $7,500. She never even realized she was placing an order as she had no clue how to use the shopping site. You can't blame Grandma because all of us have been in her place at some point or another.

It might seem convenient to swipe the credit card or opt for a BNPL scheme, but make sure you understand its implications. You don't need to take out your card for every purchase just because it seems like the easiest thing to do.

TRENDS AND HOW THEY AFFECT US

Anything that becomes a 'trend' can impact our actions. From the 'twist' in the 60s to making dalgona coffee in 2020, trends have always been part and parcel of the American lifestyle. Trends or traditions often take complicated forms and impact our decision-making process. We become reckless when it comes to following and keeping up with trends. I remember one of my dad's friends used to have an epic Halloween party every year. Everyone would go over-the-top with their costumes and there was an unsaid competition among all of them. One year, our family was going through a bit of a rough financial patch and spending on Halloween costumes was not a priority. However, my dad told my mom that they had to manage something because they could not go to the party underdressed. My mom supported him and that was when we started making our costumes ourselves. You might think that it's a small thing, but these small things define our outlook and financial sense. It took me years to realize that Halloween costumes should not be a primary concern if I am having money problems; I can show up in a simple costume and it would be completely okay.

I come from an average American family and I understand the social pressure to look the best. That is why I am particularly careful about informing you about the two most dangerous trends of our time.

I Want It Now

Whenever you are scrolling through Facebook or Instagram, you see a series of advertisements for products that you have recently looked up. Every social media platform has an algorithm that makes these customized advertisements visible to you. All brands are always trying to make you feel that you will miss out if you don't purchase it immediately. In marketing jargon it is called "instant gratification," and in normal terms we know it as 'FOMO' (fear of missing out). The psychology behind this is if you don't buy it immediately, then you are missing out on a great deal.

Whenever you shop online, you might come across something like "Only 3 left in stock. Order now." written near the description of the product. This will make you want to order it immediately because you are scared of it going out of stock. You begin to behave as if your entire life depends on that purchase and you buy it even if you are unable to afford it. Think about it, if they have only three products left in stock, they should restock. Why should you be in a hurry to buy it? This approach often makes us do unreasonable things and spend money recklessly.

Instagram Envy

My sister's daughter is 16 years old. Despite the Covid-19 restrictions, they threw her a birthday party last year. Not many people could be invited. When I reached their place, it seemed like I had come to a funeral. Amelia (my sister's daughter) was crying and my sister and her husband were arguing about something. I gave Amelia the gift and she started crying even more. The whole thing was very dramatic and I had no clue what was happening. After a while, I found out that Tracy was sad because she only got one cake while all her friends had cut multiple cakes for their birthdays despite the pandemic restrictions. She felt like she was being deprived of the things that her friends were getting. Amelia even added that her favorite Instagram influencer's parents got her a swan-shaped cake for her birthday and all she got was a regular chocolate truffle.

When I hear young people complaining about these things, it makes me feel old. I don't understand how someone can be so enamored by an Instagram influencer but I also cannot deny the fact that we are influenced by what people post on social media. Whenever you see someone buying a new car, house, or anything nice, your immediate thoughts are, *They must be doing well. I can't even afford a new phone.* Some might even feel shame or envy and decide that retail therapy will make things better.

The life that people project on Instagram is quite different from their actual life. After all the drama about cakes, Tracy wrote a very happy post about how grateful she was to her parents for arranging the lovely surprises. Everyone is putting up a show on social media, so it is unfair to compare your reality with their pretensions. Once you can get a hold of your emotions, you will be able to develop a better relationship with money and get into a healthy financial mindset.

WORKSHEET: NOTICE THE OUTSIDE NOISE

If you were checking out hats on Amazon and then you suddenly come across an advertisement for hats on Instagram, it is not the universe asking you to buy hats. The universe has other things to do than suggest hats to you. It is simply the Instagram algorithm tempting you to buy things that are on your mind. The first step to making better financial decisions is to understand the outside noises used by advertisers that are affecting you. This worksheet will help you navigate your way out of any such noises.

Questions	Your Comments Here
1. What are some of the most unlikely places where you have found advertisements for products that you were looking for?	
2. Which advertisements do you click on most? (You should note the media and the type of products that seem the most attractive to you.)	
3. Who do you compare yourself most to? What are the financial digits of such a comparison?	
4. During the last week, how many times did you feel like you were being deprived of something after you saw someone's flashy Instagram post?	
5. In the last couple of months, what were the things you bought out of impulse and regretted later?	
6. Do you often buy things that your friends are buying even if you don't want them? If yes, why do you do it?	
7. When was the last time you bought something for yourself without the influence of any outside noise?	
8. When you purchase something out of impulse, do you usually limit yourself to a specific amount? If yes, then what is that amount?	
9. Do you have the habit of hoarding things? Do you purchase things just because there is a sale? If yes, what are the things that you usually hoard?	

2

CULTIVATING YOUR MONEY
MINDSET

The most important thing is the decision to act, the rest is merely tenacity.
–Amelia Earhart

My friend Sarah and I were talking the other day. She came to me asking for some financial advice since she was in significant debt. I always knew she had an obsession with online shopping but I never realized that it had become so much worse. Whenever she felt upset or sad, she would buy something to lift her mood. This slowly grew into an addiction and she tried to hide it from her husband because she knew what she was doing wasn't right. Things had gotten out of control and now she owes a fortune in credit card bills.

I'm still not sure how to help Sarah but her situation got me thinking about this mentality. Sarah kept saying things like, "Buying those shoes was the only good thing about my life at that point." It's not just her. Many of us link our self-esteem and happiness with buying and owning things. People tend to indulge in desserts or a glass of wine more frequently than they should; it's the same with money. Reckless spending habits cultivate an unhealthy money mindset which has a direct impact on your financial situation. Budgeting is not enough. You need to look at yourself deeply to understand why you behave a particular way when it comes to money.

DO YOU NEED MONEY TO BE HAPPY?

The question might seem philosophical or too broad but have you ever asked yourself: *Can money buy you happiness?* When I put this question in front of you what I am actually asking is, does your happiness directly correlate with the size of your bank balance?

I decided to go to university to pursue higher studies. All my friends had taken up full-time jobs by then and I always felt a little left behind. I was frustrated because I did not have a real job and education was taking up most of my time. Later on, after I graduated and got a job, I was very pleased with myself because I was earning money. However, there was still a sense of unfulfilled desire within myself as many of my friends were earning a lot more than me.

Is There a Magic Figure?

Turns out, there is. A study conducted by psychologist Daniel Kahneman and economist Angus Deaton (2010) revealed that an annual income of $75,000 was the limit up to which happiness was directly proportional to salary. This means that you will continue to feel happy as your salary increases till it reaches $75,000. After that point, your emotional well-being or how you feel daily will not change because you know that you are earning enough money. However, the study also stated that your overall satisfaction of life will keep on increasing even after you have reached the $75,000 limit. The psychology behind this is that initially, a pay raise will keep you happy until you get used to being around money. When you realize that you have enough to sustain yourself, your focus will shift to your overall quality of life.

It's All Relative

My mother always used to tell me, "Your biggest competition is you. You should try to outdo yourself every time." This is an idealistic lesson to impart, but most of the time we compete with our friends, colleagues, or any other acquaintance and measure ourselves in terms of their progress. My niece Amelia was crying over cake and her birthday party not being as fancy as her friends'. However, she was not satisfied with the fact that she had received AirPods, an iPad, and keys to a car which she would be driving once she obtained her permit. Most of us do not notice all the good things in our lives because we are very busy comparing ourselves with others. It is not ideal, but it is what it is. No matter how much money you earn, you might unreasonably feel that you are poor if you see someone else earning more than you.

Purpose Is What We Seek

Most of us often make the mistake of thinking that money is the only thing that matters while looking for a job. I took up my first job with a similar attitude. The workload was tremendous and the hours were long, but I never complained because the pay was very good. To me, that was the only important part. However, as time passed I realized how unhappy I was in my current situation. I was making good money, but it seemed like I had no purpose. I was working very hard but I was not happy because the work did not satisfy my intellectual and emotional needs. That was when I realized that job satisfaction and a sense of direction are very important in one's career.

Feeling like you are engaging in rewarding work puts you in a headspace that even the biggest paycheck you can get won't measure up to. However, would you be willing to switch your high-paying meaningless job with a low-paying job that gives you a sense of purpose? No, and that is why human emotions are complex. We have a very complicated relationship with money and often fail to understand how to deal with it.

SPENDING HABITS AND THEIR IMPLICATIONS

You thought only machines could be automatic? Well, you will be surprised to know that our habits make us do many things mechanically. It is a proven scientific process which automates many of our behaviors. This might happen unconsciously or as a result of somebody's intentions. During the lockdown phase of the Covid-19 pandemic, most people fell into a habit of sleeping late and waking up late because there was no fixed routine. However, most habits can be changed over time with structured efforts. This means that even if you are a night-owl, that doesn't mean you can't change yourself into a morning person over time.

Spending habits are similar to the other habits that you have. Most of the time we do not pay attention, but small habits can have a big impact on your financial situation. For instance, you might be a hopeless romantic who loves to make grand gestures for your dates. But the problem is that your dates change too much and occur too frequently. Whenever you go out on a date, you buy fancy flowers and chocolates. If you go on three dates in a month, just imagine how much you are spending on flowers. Being a romantic is fine as long as it does not burn a giant bouquet-sized hole in your pocket.

Examples of Spending Habits

Once you form a habit, you do not even realize that it's involuntary. Your behavior with money remains constant in a given set of situations. The best example of a spending habit is spending a lot of money on the day you get paid. Maybe you wish-list a few things on Amazon and order them the moment you get paid. You may also like to take your family out to dinner or order takeout. It's a common habit to spend money on payday because you feel like you deserve to be rewarded for all the hard work you put in.

More such habits include buying souvenirs while on vacation or waiting until the last moment to book flight tickets. Another important example of a spending habit is spending money on people you love. Many parents do it for their children as a sign of their unconditional love. I do it for my pets. I buy toys and treats for them whenever I get a chance. Most of the time they don't care about the toys or refuse to touch the treats, because that's how pets are. Although I am well aware of this, I still end up spending on them. I believe that I am spoiling them with goodies when in reality I am indulging myself. This is not an ideal situation, but as long as it's not hurting you, a little self-indulgence can be healthy.

How Are Spending Habits Formed?

Like most of our other habits, our spending patterns are hugely influenced by our parents. When I say this, I don't mean that your spending habits will be exactly like your folks', and it can be something completely different as well because you never agreed to their way of handling money. They can also be influenced by your spouse or other significant people in your life.

Our culture and surroundings play a significant role in shaping our spending habits. In some cultures, weddings and social functions are very lavishly celebrated while others believe in keeping it simple, no matter how important the occasion is. People all over the world have different perceptions about their way of life which is why spending habits vary widely among different cultures. Religious beliefs are also an important factor because many religions focus a lot on the importance of charity. Some people might be donating money even if they are not doing well financially.

We are all wired differently and two people from the same family can have very different spending habits. Despite growing up in the same house and having the same upbringing, my sister and I have a completely different outlook toward money. I have slowly grown into a cautious spender and think a million times before making a small purchase while my sister is the exact opposite. She is impulsive and buys random, expensive things without giving it a second thought. (No wonder I am the family favorite.)

The media also encourages certain spending habits in us because advertisers are always pushing a consumerist agenda. For instance, teenage girls going crazy over the multiple-step skincare regime seen on TikToc or Youtube." So they buy cleansers, toners, serums, moisturizers, and day creams. This obsession has created a spending habit where young girls are made to think they are 'investing' in their skin.

CHANGING YOUR MONEY MINDSET

Spending habits can become problematic if you are not careful. An unhealthy spending pattern is the biggest contributor to financial stress and worry. My friend Sarah suffers from chronic anxiety and depression because of her impulsive shopping tendencies. Money is the key to a peaceful life but it can also wreak havoc if you do not know how to manage it. Since you are wired in a certain way and can't seem to shake off our spending habits, you get scared and anxious. These are some of the common fears that you may experience if you can't keep track of real-life spending habits:

- Insufficient savings: Most people are scared that they do

not have enough money saved in case of an emergency or for their retirement. In America, this is a genuine concern as we already learned that most Americans do not have the financial means to afford $400. Middle-aged people whose kids are in school also worry whether they will be able to support them and provide for their higher education. Many people have ailing parents and taking care of them can become a financial burden if they don't have a fund.

- Job concerns: If you tend to spend more than what you can afford, you are bound to be scared about your employment situation. You will constantly be anxious about what will happen if you lose your job.

- Discussing money with your significant other: Whenever we know we have done something wrong, we tend to hide it from our parents or partners. This is a childlike instinct that is present in all of us even as adults. Sarah has a shopping addiction but she cannot share the same with her husband because of fear of judgment. Money is a difficult topic to discuss with your partner and it becomes even more uncomfortable if you know you are bad at handling it.

- Inability to pay bills or get out of debt: A very common financial worry that most people have is the inability to pay bills within the stipulated time. If you are someone who spends a lot of money on credit cards, getting out of debt is also a legit concern. The average American has a student loan, car loan, and credit card dues which can become a lot if not managed properly.

- Poor credit score: Debt is like a vicious cycle. If you have too much credit card debt then you will not be able to afford a mortgage. If you miss even one repayment, it can seriously hamper your credit score which will make you ineligible for further credit. This is a financial worry that troubles many people.

- Inability to afford health insurance: Health insurance is an absolute necessity because healthcare is extremely expensive without it in America. Somebody with an unhealthy spending habit is bound to be worried about not being able to afford health insurance because they might have spent the money elsewhere.
- Having to declare bankruptcy: Declaring bankruptcy is always the last resort. If someone is having financial problems, they will be scared of this happening.

Change the Habits and Break the Cycle

J.K. Rowling wrote in one of the Harry Potter books: "Help will always be given at Hogwarts to those who ask for it." This is a mantra that you should always follow in real life, especially when dealing with your finances. When you have an unhealthy spending habit, the world might seem like a dark and lonely place because you are unable to confide in anyone. However, you are not as alone as you think. The first step is to ask for help and the best person who can help you is you. You have to be confident that you are capable of helping yourself and pulling yourself out of any financial mess. Here are a few tips to get started:

- Our inboxes are filled with emails from various shopping websites that inform us about upcoming sales and other promotional offers. Take some time out one day and unsubscribe from all such emails that tempt you to make impulsive purchases. Out of sight, out of mind is more effective than you can imagine.
- Unfollow people and posts on social media that intimidate you, tempt you and make you feel like you are

being deprived. There are many people who specifically post pictures to project their 'awesome' life. If you are unable to feel happy for them, then don't blame yourself. I would suggest you fill your social media with things that make do make you happy. It can be art, stories, or endless dog videos. Just make sure that you are mentally satisfied because we make the worst financial decisions when we are upset.

- When you go shopping, estimate how much you will spend and take only cash with you. This will prevent you from overspending or swiping your credit card when you don't need to.

- If you are someone who has kids, refrain from bringing them along when you go shopping. Kids often pick out random stuff and we end up indulging them. The small things add up and your grocery bill becomes much more than you thought it would be.

- Don't rush into buying anything right after seeing an advertisement. My advice is to sleep on it and if you still want that thing after a week, then you are free to purchase it. Impulse is often the driving factor for buying anything and it's best to wait it out before making the purchase.

- Try to start saving some money. No amount is small but you have to start somewhere to reach your destination. Remember that this is a process and keep tracking your expenses until you can start saving. Be kind to yourself if you are unable to reach your goal immediately.

I understand that spending habits can become a pattern that is very hard to break. I had my share of problems while dealing with these habits but I have managed to control my impulses by preparing a budget and sticking to it. Making mistakes is a part of the self-improvement process but you need to make sure that you aren't repeating the same mistakes. Having a sense of financial direction is very important if you want to take control of your spending habits—and this is where a budget will be extremely helpful.

WORKSHEET: TAKE A LOOK AT YOUR MONEY HABITS

In this activity, you will be performing a self-assessment of your spending and saving habits. The purpose behind this activity is for you to reflect upon your problematic financial behaviors and make necessary changes.

Questions	Your Comments Here
What are your subconscious spending habits? • When do you spend the most money? (For example, it could be when you are out with friends, while you are scrolling through social media, or when you are in a mall.) • Have you ever noticed your mood while you are shopping? Are you happy, depressed, or simply bored?	
Where do you spend money consciously? • What are the expenses that you are aware of? • Did you remember to include rent and debt repayments? • Which of these payments are automated? • Are you aware of the automated payments?	
How many promotional emails do you receive in a week? How many of these emails have made you purchase something in the last couple of months?	
What are your plans for the future with your current spending and saving habits?	
When do you experience the greatest temptation to spend money? In the last couple of months, how many times have you given in to the temptation? When you gave in, what did you buy?	
What is one monetary habit that you wish to get rid of and why?	

STEP 1—TAKE THE GUESSWORK OUT OF BUDGETING

Beware of little expenses, a small leak will sink a great ship. –Benjamin Franklin

It was almost Christmas and Alex could finally take some time out to go shopping for his family. He had a big family and he loved to buy gifts for them. He went to the mall because everything is available in one place and he wouldn't have to hop from one area to another. After he was done, Alex was surprised to find how much money he had spent. He didn't have any cash left and had to buy the last gifts with his credit card. He was freaking out because his credit card dues were already quite high and he could barely manage to pay the minimum amount each month.

Alex is not an exception because we often go overboard while shopping and then regret it later. When you have a lot of financial obligations, managing all of them can become overwhelming which is why you need to have a well-defined plan. After considering the statutory liabilities (like your debts), you have to fix up amounts which you are allowed to spend on other heads. This is not a game of monopoly where things depend on luck. You have to take control of your finances, which is where a budget figures in.

PREPARING A BUDGET

Your partner comes home from work and lets you know that you know that their colleagues will be coming over for dinner next Saturday. You feel a bit annoyed but you like cooking so you agree, but your partner cannot confirm how many people will be coming. In this situation, is it possible for you to start your preparations? How will you manage something you cannot measure?

Personal financial management is similar to this situation. If you do not have a proper understanding of your finances, you will be trying to build a shaky foundation. This poses the next important question: Where do you begin?

What Is a Budget?

Before getting into the details about preparing a budget, try to understand what it means. A budget is a summary of your income and expenses for a specified period of time. Companies usually prepare their budgets for a quarter or a year. In personal finance, the time horizon is usually a month. It is a kind of plan which helps you track your expenses in comparison to your income and reflect upon your financial situation.

People often compare budgets with diets; they're hard to stick to and restrictive. However, if you have the correct tools, understand the rationale and keep enough wiggle-room for some 'cheat' moments, budgets can become your greatest asset in personal finance. Dieting or budgeting, the key to being successful is to keep it realistic and understand your situation. If you have to stay mentally or physically active throughout the day, a "juice cleanse" might not be the sensible option. Similarly, if you have many financial obligations, you might not always be able to save as much as you are supposed to. The point is, you should not be rigid while preparing a budget and don't try something which seems impossible. A flexible and organized budget will make financial management smoother.

Set Your Budget

Since a budget is essentially a financial plan, the first thing you have to do while setting it up is make a list of your income and all your expenses for the chosen period. Preparing a budget becomes very simple if you follow these steps:

Gather Your Paperwork

It might not sound like much, but gathering your paperwork is very important while preparing a budget. Most of us are careless about it because all bills and forms are now accessed online. I remember my dad used to arrange all his documents inside a file so that he could access them anytime he wanted. Needless to say, he was good with money. None of us have such files now because everything is paperless. My tip would be to create a folder on your laptop or computer, download all the relevant documents, and save it there. The documents that you need to keep handy are:

- Bank statements for the concerned period. If your budget period is a month, then you must have bank statements of all your accounts during that month.
- Investment accounts. If you have made any new investments that month, make sure to include details of the same. You won't be investing every month, so keep a record of your existing investments and account for any recurring contributions you might be making.

27

- Recent utility bills. This will generally include bills for gas, electricity, sewage, and garbage disposal. However, there are many additional utilities that you spend on every month, like phone and internet bills.
- W-2s and paystubs if you work as a salaried employee and 1099s if you work as an independent contractor. These are important documents and proof that you have earned money during the specified period.
- Credit card bills. The credit card company usually sends you a monthly statement indicating how much you have spent and the minimum amount that you have to pay.
- A record of all the receipts that you have. You can have more than one source of income or you might have sold some assets and earned cash from the sale.
- Statements of all the loans that you currently have. This can include your mortgage, auto loan, and student loan documents.

The objective of gathering these documents is to keep a tab on your income and expenses. We often forget to include the little things which eventually add up and become bigger. For instance, you pay for Netflix every month but there is a high chance that you forgot to include it in your utility bills because it doesn't seem like a traditional 'utility' bill to you.

Calculate Your Income

If you are employed in a company and you receive fixed pay every week, then you have to consider the net pay (after deducting taxes). In case you are self-employed, consider payments that you receive from all your contracts and other sources like child support, social security, or alimony. If you work as a freelancer or have varying income every month, take your lowest pay during the last 6-month period as your base income.

Calculate Your Expenses

Noting down your monthly expenses is essential for a good budget plan. Dig deep and try to calculate all your expenses every month. Some common expenses include:

- Loan repayments
- Rent and other utility bills
- Insurance
- Children's education
- Groceries and other essential items
- Transportation costs
- Personal care, grooming, and entertainment
- Savings

Look at your bank and credit card statements and search for expenses that you might be incurring irregularly. For instance, I purchase a 15 lb pack of cat food every couple of months. This is a regular expense but it does not appear every month which is why it is important to make provisions for the same in your monthly budget.

Classify Your Expenses

Your expenses can be classified broadly into two heads—fixed and variable. Fixed expenses are those that remain fixed every month like loan repayments, utility bills, or any other bills. Variable expenses change every month like groceries, gas, or entertainment. When you classify your expenses, you will understand how much some of them vary each month. For example, if you see that your restaurant bills drastically increase in some months, you can identify a pattern and make necessary changes.

Compare Your Income and Expenses

Once you have gathered all the information related to your income and expenses, make a comparison of the two. If your income is higher than your expenses, then you are in a good position. In case you are not and the cash flow comes to be negative, you have to take a look at your expenses and consider which areas can be adjusted. Your budget should not be rigid and you should keep updating it as your situations change.

USING YOUR BUDGET OPTIMALLY

In the previous chapter we talked about the importance of having a positive money mindset to reach your financial goals. Preparing a budget is a continuation of that mentality. You have to first understand the importance of a budget so that you don't feel the temptation to splurge on unnecessary things.

Everyone has a set of long-term goals and priorities. You might want to purchase your dream car or a house. A budget provides direction to your dreams and helps you stay focused. When you prepare a budget, you have a visual representation of your financial condition. You might have had an impression that you are poor, but your budget can show you that you are simply spending too much on groceries or restaurants. Moreover, since you delve deep into your finances while preparing a budget, it points out those expenses which you cannot afford. For example, when you analyze your credit card dues you might find extravagant purchases that are beyond your means. Preparing a budget also helps you to shed light on your actual financial position and in turn motivates you to prepare yourself for emergencies. In today's economic climate, this is of utmost importance because everything is so uncertain right now. Who would have thought that we will have to go through a deadly pandemic and months of lockdown? So many people suddenly found themselves without a job or suffered severe pay cuts. People who have a solid emergency fund are the ones who could survive the financial aftermath of the pandemic.

The first time I prepared a budget, I was surprised to find how many unnecessary expenses I make every month. For example, I paid for a cable subscription that had over 500 channels while my husband and I watched the same five channels on repeat. When I casually mentioned my grocery bill to my neighbor one day, she told me that the store I bought from had a record of overcharging their customers. I had just moved into the neighborhood and had no clue about anything and I selected the store because the owner seemed nice. As I learned to analyze my expenses, I started to think of ways to cut back on extra things. I learned to compare prices before buying anything. Budgeting helped me come out of my comfort zones and look for alternatives.

Prioritize Your Budget

You have to first figure out your financial objectives that you want to achieve with the help of your budget. Having a sense of clarity is very important since budgeting can be overwhelming and there are many elements taking you in a million different directions. The main objective of budgeting is to stay on top of your finances, but what should the order of priorities be? Let's find out.

- Whatever your long-term or short-term financial goals may be, your priority should be planning for retirement rather than saving. After you retire, your income won't be as much as it is now and you need to have a steady inflow of cash in order to maintain your lifestyle. Even if your employer contributes to the 401(k), you must do your part to maintain the fund. You can start by matching your employer's contribution and look for other ways to save as well.

- Next, your budget must be designed in a way to pay off high-interest debts. This is usually your credit card debt and you must make provisions to repay it at the earliest because interest payments can eat up all your savings.
- Your budget must allow you to create an emergency fund so that you have a financial backup in case of any unfortunate incident.
- When you are budgeting, you should also make provisions for expected costs like simple repairs and maintenance costs. These are not big emergencies, but regular things that are bound to happen. If you make provisions for these expenses, it will not hamper your regular savings.

Create Some Savings

To use your budget optimally, you should prepare your budget in such a way so that it helps you to save enough money. You already know that no matter what your intentions are, savings should always be a big priority in your budget. When you have a proper system, saving money becomes much easier even if your income is not very high. When your income and expenses are almost the same, saving money often becomes a challenge which is why certain proven methods will help you in reaching your savings goals.

The 50/30/20 Rule

When you start the budgeting process, you will find that saving money is more difficult than it seems. The burden of our financial responsibilities is so heavy that we fail to prioritize savings. We know its importance, but we can't get around to the execution which is why you must follow a fixed pattern and classify your expenses properly. The 50/30/20 rule is great for beginners who are having trouble allocating the right amount to the right heads. This rule states that you should be spending 50% of your income on essential items or 'needs.' These are the things which you cannot live without like groceries and basic utilities. This category will also include unavoidable statutory payments like mortgage, auto loan payment, credit card bills, and other obligations. Next, you will allocate 30% of your income for non-essential things or 'wants' which include expenses for eating out, vacations, sports or concert tickets, or any other luxurious purchase that you make. When both your needs and wants are taken care of, you can dedicate 20% of your income to savings. This money will be contributed to your emergency fund, IRA, or any other retirement fund, or you can simply save it for purchasing an asset like a house.

The biggest benefit of the 50/30/20 rule is that it gives you room for having fun. In the beginning, your motivation level will be at the highest but it will begin to shake as time passes. You need to permit yourself to indulge so that you can continue the process. I have heard many people complain, "I have no money for myself. Everything is going to savings!" This sounds like a ridiculous complaint because the money is being kept for future use but people have the tendency to become illogical and even hysterical when they are unable to get what they want. Mentally we are all still children who fuss when they are not given their favorite toy. When your inner child is happy, the adult inside you can peacefully deal with the savings.

Budgeting Hacks

Budgeting is not rocket science and you can customize it according to your needs. In my experience, I have discovered the following hacks that you might find useful while you start the budgeting process:

- If you are a freelancer or work on commission, there are high chances that your income will be inadequate during certain periods. In such cases, you should save aggressively when you are earning well so that you can cover yourself later on. Budgeting in a variable income is very tricky but freelancers often make more money than salaried people. The problem is that they are unable to manage the money due to a lack of an institutional framework. Let the budget be your anchor and it will help you stay afloat in the slow periods.
- In today's life, a cash-only budget can seem unrealistic. Especially after the pandemic, many stores accept only contactless payments. However, credit cards and other digital payment methods make us spend more. Find out the areas in which you tend to overspend and have a cash-only policy for them. For example, if you buy too many clothes, try to have a cash budget for it and make sure you don't exceed it.
- Use your credit card only when it is essential. Interest can mount up on your bill and you might not be able to afford it at the end of the month. Even better, get rid of your credit card or at the very least, lower the limit of your credit card to as low as you can.
- If you are not good with numbers and spreadsheets freak you out, use budgeting software to prepare your budget. Install an easy app on your phone which will help you to

    track your expenses and will give you reminders when you are overspending.
- For most people, fast food is one of the biggest areas of spending because they might be too busy to cook or have no idea how to plan meals. A menu planning service might be able to help you in figuring out how to cook and what ingredients are needed for the process.

Great things happen to people who stretch themselves thin, but not so much that it breaks you to pieces. The biggest factor that makes a budget successful is how you feel about it. If your budget makes you feel negative or poor about your situation, then you won't find the motivation to go on with it. You have to feel excited about your budget and not think of it as an inconvenience. This attitude will help you accustom yourself to a financial plan and will inspire you to do better every time. Your budget will be the base of your entire financial management process which is why it is important to enjoy it and get it right. This will set things in motion and make saving money easier for you.

WORKSHEET: ESTABLISH YOUR BUDGET

In this worksheet, I will assist you in preparing a budget. Everything looks good in theory but we mess it up when we are about to implement it. That is why I have taken extra care to make sure that you do it right. Budgeting will become easier when you fill out the following format:

Budget for the month of _____, 202_	
Income:	$$$$
Salary income	
Income from any other source	
Any unexpected receipt	
Total Income:	
Expenses:	
Housing expenses	
Rent or mortgage	
Homeowners or renter's insurance	
Utilities (electric, gas, cable, sewage, etc)	
Taxes	
Food	
Groceries	
Takeout or restaurant	
Health	
Doctors' fees	
Health insurance	
Medicine	
Transportation	

Gas	
Public transport costs	
Car maintenance costs	
Car loan	
Debts	
Credit card bills	
Student debt	
Any other loans	
Miscellaneous expenses	
Child Support	
Alimony	
Any money paid to family members	
Any professional consultancy fees paid	
Any new Purchases (For example clothes or gadgets)	
Savings/Investments	
Contributions to IRA	
Contributions to any other savings plan	
Systematic investment plan contribution	
Any other investments	
Total Expenses:	
Calculate the difference between Total Income and Total Expenses to find out your cash flow.	

4

STEP 2—SAVE SIMPLY AND EASILY

When prosperity comes, do not use all of it. –Confucius

My husband and I like a debate, some may call it an argument. When we first got married, we debated a lot because we were starting everything from scratch. One day we were fighting about who fights more. Naturally, each of us blamed the other. So, we decided to put an end to this controversy through a carefully curated method: Each of us took a jar and decided that every time one of us initiated a 'debate', the other would put $10 in their own jar. After a month we would check who had more money in their jar and it would be decided once and for all who is the bigger culprit. If his jar had more, that would mean I have started more fights and vice versa. Both of us followed this religiously and in a couple of months, both of our jars were stacked with $10 bills. We ended up having a major laugh when we discovered this and never bothered to check whose jar had more money again. Incidentally, this was a time in our lives when we were facing a bit of a cash crunch and were unable to save much. This was an unexpected treasure for us and made us realize that saving money is not as difficult as it seems. We might need to change our outlook and find creative ways to start saving.

IMPORTANCE OF SAVINGS

There are a million examples and real-life stories that depict the importance of savings. You won't find a single person who claims that they are sorry because they saved money. Even hibernating animals keep resources saved up so that they can consume them during the winter months when food is not easily available. Saving money should be your most important financial goal. For peace of mind, a guideline for the amount of savings, is to be able to cover six months of ALL expenses. I think it would be prudent to have a year's worth of expenses covered especially now we are living in a more uncertain world. If you are still not convinced, here are a few reasons that establish the importance of savings:

- It provides you with a sense of security. Life is uncertain. One minute you are sipping margaritas by the beach and the next moment you might be in the isolation ward of a hospital. Adequate savings will help you face these unexpected situations with ease because you will have financial backup. You don't always have to assume the worst; savings will help you get through any kind of emergency comfortably. Suppose your parents live across the country and your mother suddenly falls sick. They have the financial means to support themselves but your mother wants you to come and visit her. You have to book a last minute flight to reach as soon as possible. These tickets are usually the most expensive and can become a burden if you do not have enough savings.
- Have you ever heard of the term "golden handcuffs?" This is when someone is trapped in a job that they don't

like but cannot quit because it pays so well. Many people think about leaving their jobs because they feel like they are destined to do something else. If you have enough savings to support yourself, you can think about leaving that job and pursuing your dream. When you are taking the time to figure things out, your savings will ensure that you continue to have a comfortable life.

- Financial problems are the biggest contributors to conflict in personal relationships. Many marriages have fallen apart over money matters. That is why you need to have enough money saved up to have a peaceful personal life. It is okay to expect your partner's support through a financial crisis, but it is best if you can avoid such unpleasant situations. Money problems affect children to a great extent because they feel like they are being deprived. Many of them blame themselves because their parents have to spend money on them. A sound financial backup will ensure a healthy environment and proper education for your children. If you can save enough money, you can even leave a legacy for the next generation or help others in your family in times of need.

- Most of us have intentions to make big purchases like a house or a car. Even if you are eligible for a mortgage, you have to pay a certain percentage as a down payment when you buy a house. This is a lot of money and you won't be able to afford it unless you save the money for it.

- Money is the biggest reason why so many of us suffer from stress and anxiety. We are constantly worried because we feel we do not have enough money to afford all the things we want and pay all bills on time. When you have adequate savings, you can eliminate these worries and start living your life peacefully.

WHERE ARE YOU GOING WRONG?

Despite the current economic turmoil, most people tend to be ignorant when it comes to savings. According to a 2016 GO Banking Rates Survey, 69% of Americans have less than $1,000 in their savings accounts (Elkins, 2016). Many people are clueless about retirement accounts which means that they have no idea how they would support themselves financially once they stop working. This implies two things—either people do not know about saving money or they do not care about it, both of which are extremely dangerous. This attitude can lead you into severe financial distress if you are not careful about it.

Signs That You Are Not Saving Enough Money

It is important understand your situation correctly to be able to manage your finances more efficiently. If you experience one or more of the following signs, then you are not saving enough:

You Are Clueless About How Much You Are Spending

Usually we are aware of how much we earn. Be it a fixed paycheck or freelance income, we know how much is coming in. However, if you do not have a clear picture of your expenses, then you are spending more than you think. Starbucks every other day, a premium Netflix subscription, and many other things add up to create a big list of unnoticed expenses. Somebody unaware of their expenses can never be saving enough.

Your Savings Goals Are Undefined

All financially stable people have one thing in common—they are very specific and organized about money. If you do not have specific savings goals, you can never be saving enough money. There are many unexplored areas in your financial plan which might broaden your scope to save. Savings goals can be big or small, but they must be realistic and achievable. To understand your savings goals better, you must assess your life and what you want from it in the near future. Do you plan to get married soon? If you are married, are you keen on starting a family in the next couple of years? Do you want to purchase a house? Do you want to start your business? Your personal and professional life is the biggest indicator of your financial priorities, which in turn define your savings goals.

You Live Paycheck To Paycheck

Suppose you got paid on Thursday this week. Right after the money is credited, you have to make several statutory payments. You pay some of them and delay the others till next week because you have barely any money left to get through the week. If this is your financial situation, then you are living paycheck to paycheck. It is impossible to have any savings in such a scenario.

You Are Delaying Retirement Savings

You keep thinking that you are now too young to be thinking about boring stuff like retirement. The truth is, it is never too early to plan retirement savings. It freaks you out to think about the distant future because deep inside your heart you know you do not have enough money to save for life after you stop working. You don't want to think about it and that is why you keep putting it off.

You Don't Have the Money to Start Investing

Savings and investment go hand in hand. If you do not have

enough money to invest, then you haven't saved enough money. People usually start investing when they have met their immediate savings goals like creating an emergency fund. You can't even think about investing money if you don't have savings to cover any unexpected costs.

You Can't Pay Your Credit Card Bills In Full

If you use credit cards because you don't have enough cash, then you are far behind on your savings goals. You struggle to pay the minimum due every month because your expenses are greater than your income.

You Don't Have An Emergency Fund

Not having an emergency fund is the biggest and most important indicator of inadequate savings. This is an undesirable situation where you are barely making ends meet.

The Problematic Attitude

Most Americans struggle to save money even if they are earning a good amount because of a lack of financial knowledge. However, ignorance is not the only reason behind that. Many people associate savings with making major sacrifices or having to give up everything fun, just as they associate budgets with restriction. You might hear someone say, "I had to give up my trip to Disneyland because of that stupid savings plan." They are only focusing on the trip when the money that they saved will eventually be used to buy a new house.

You are not depriving yourself of anything when you set money aside for savings. You are actually securing your future and building a financial foundation for yourself and your family. If you eat an entire cheesecake before Thanksgiving dinner, then you won't be able to enjoy the turkey or any of the other special dishes. Giving up the cheesecake is not a sacrifice, it is a logical decision.

HOW TO START SAVING MONEY

When you are used to dealing with money in a certain way, you might find it difficult to suddenly start saving. Don't worry, we will go over each step carefully so that you can understand what to do.

Since you already know the basics of budgeting, take a look at all your expenses. Saving money from your existing financial situation implies that you have to cut back on some expenses. Eliminate the fixed expenses because you cannot change them. Look at the variable expenses, particularly the ones which are most expensive, and try to figure out where you can cut back.

As mentioned, most financial experts suggest that you have savings worth three to six months of living expenses (I prefer a year, but let's start with a goal of three months and build on this). This might seem like a tall target, which is why it is important to define your savings goals first. Make a list of all the purchases or other financial goals that you wish to achieve in the short term and long term. Take some time to brainstorm all the different areas that your savings will be directed to.

If you are starting from zero, then your first target should be to create an emergency fund worth $1,000. Once you have achieved that target, make regular contributions to increase that fund after you are done with your debt repayments. You should build an emergency fund before repaying some of your debts because uncertain situations can arise at any time. However, a priority should always be clearing your credit card debt due to fees associated.

To save money more effectively, you have to consider both long-term major strategies and short-term minor strategies.

Minor Short-Term Changes to Make

As I keep saying, the little things are the ones that matter the most when it comes to managing your money. It goes beyond turning off the thermostat or inflating your tires. Make these small changes in your daily life and watch your savings grow.

Look at Underused/Unused Subscriptions

I can already feel your guilt as you recall all the times you have skipped the gym. However, you are not the only one whose gym membership is unused, so don't beat yourself up about it. Instead, cancel the membership and start working out at home. You can easily do squats or push-ups in your backyard. You can consult the countless free workout videos available on YouTube to get it right. Those of you who work out with weights can invest in a weight set one time when you can afford it. Having said that, if working out is an important part of your life, then you might not want to cancel the gym membership and look for some other subscriptions which you are not using. Most of us have subscriptions to Amazon Prime, Netflix, Hulu, Apple Music, Spotify, and many other streaming services. After working around 35 hours a week, how much time do you have left to watch so many movies on so many platforms? Even if you are a movie buff or binge-watcher, you know you can give up one or two subscriptions. If you are paying for more than one music streaming platform, you should stop immediately because music is the same everywhere. Moreover, all songs are available for free on YouTube so you might want to rethink your streaming priorities.

Time Your Purchases

Online shopping platforms and physical stores have many sales throughout the year that allow you to buy things at a significantly lesser price. If you are planning to make a big purchase like a car or any big electronic device, you can consider timing it around December since most companies are desperate to meet their year-end quotas. Most websites give huge discounts during the Black Friday Sale around Thanksgiving.

Use Coupons

There are many apps like Dosh, Ibotta, and Honey which provide coupons to retail outlets, groceries, and hotels that will help you to save money on your purchases. Most of these apps provide digital coupons so there is no need for any physical papers.

Look at What You Are Eating

This advice is not limited to dieting. We spend most of our money on food and not all of it is essential. You must plan your meals before going to the grocery store so that you buy only the things that you need. Look for the generic and inexpensive items on the top and bottom shelves since it is every store's marketing policy to display the most expensive items in the middle. Another interesting tip revealed by marketing psychologists is that we tend to overspend when we go to the store hungry, so you might want to note that as well. Americans waste a lot of food which implies a waste of money. Take note of all the food you have purchased and which of them went bad because you could not use it. We often bulk up on groceries because of the discounts, but there is no point if you end up throwing it away. Don't buy milk or milk products in large quantities since they go bad very fast.

Track how many times you eat out during the week. Many working people like to eat their lunch in restaurants. If you are one of those people, try to bring home-cooked meals instead because you will be saving a lot of money that way.

Share Services

If you don't like the idea of canceling your streaming subscriptions, find friends who are willing to share them with you. Both of you will be paying a lower price and it would be a win-win situation. Sharing is also economical when you carpool to work or school. Opt for thrift stores and sell those clothes which you don't use anymore.

Think Long Before Buying

When you are buying something expensive, think how much time it will take you to earn that money. This will help you understand the true value of that item.

Major Long-Term Changes

The small changes might make a big difference eventually, but you need to implement major changes if you wish to increase your savings exponentially. Apart from matching your employer's contribution to the 401(k), these are the following steps you can take:

Automate Your Savings

You might forget to deposit your savings every month which is why it is a good idea to automate the process. Most banks offer the option to automatically deduct a specified amount of money every month on a certain date. This will make saving money a part of your financial management system.

Apply the 30-day Rule

Before making an extravagant purchase, wait 30 days. If you still think the purchase is justified, go for it.

Review Your Regular Plans

Consider switching to a cheaper cell phone plan after checking how much data you use. Review your cable and internet plans as well and check for bundle offers. Check your existing insurance plans and compare cheaper alternatives.

Refinance Your Loans

When you refinance a loan, your monthly repayment is reduced due to lower interest rates and you get various other benefits as well. You can refinance your mortgage, auto loan, or any other debt you have.

Assess and Utilize Your Bank Accounts

Once we get used to a bank, we usually don't feel like switching. However, banks are always coming up with competitive offers and interest rates and you must take advantage of it. Keep your savings account separate so you don't end up borrowing from it and go for high-yield securities for long-term investments. Parents must make use of 529s, ESAs, and College Savings Accounts and start saving early for their child's education.

Most of us are constantly worried about the many expenses that we have to incur. Savings help us create a financial foundation which is like having a safety net that will always be there in case of any emergency. When you have a grip over your savings, you will feel confident exploring other areas of personal finance. With enough money in your bank, you can finally start thinking about repaying all those debts.

WORKSHEET: CREATE YOUR SAVINGS GOALS

Once you have identified your various financial goals, including savings, it is time to get into action. In this worksheet, we will take a look at what needs to be done to achieve these goals.

Directions	Your Comments Here
Write down all your financial goals (like buying a car or a house, repaying certain debts, etc.) and the amount required to achieve that goal. Then write down when you want to achieve it. Set a realistic time frame. For example: Saving for the down payment of a house. Amount: $20,000 Time Frame: 5 years	
After you have made the list, prioritize the goals.	
Once you have prioritized your goals, you know which ones are most important. Based on your financial situation, try to gauge whether you can fully achieve one goal before moving to the next one. You can also choose to take small steps and make steady progress in all your goals.	
Write down five minor short-term changes and three major long-term changes that you made or are planning to make to achieve your savings goals.	
Track your progress after a couple of months to check how you are doing.	

5

STEP 3—MANAGE YOUR DEBT
LIKE A PRO

Debt is a social and ideological construct, not a simple economic fact.
–Noam Chomsky

The other day I was invited to my friend Dave's son's third birthday party. Dave was my college friend and we stayed in touch. While we were chatting, he received a call and came back around 15 minutes later. Dave's wife was giving him questioning looks when he told her that it was the bank calling about the student loan. I was curious and asked Dave how he could need a student loan now when his son was only three. Dave replied that it was his student loan that he was referring to. This got me thinking. We left college more than a decade ago and Dave was still servicing his student debt. Most student loans have a tenure of 10 years and if Dave had still not repaid it, he must have refinanced it or opted for some kind of restructuring. It seemed unusual because Dave seemed financially stable—and yet he was struggling with his debts.

Debts are an essential part of every economy. It drives the

financial system and promotes overall economic growth. Everyone you know is living with some kind of debt and most of them are not equipped to handle it. Since there is no way around debt, we should learn to manage it properly.

GOOD VS BAD DEBT

Debts freak us out and we tend to look at it like it is Thanos in our personal finance journey. Yet you cannot deny that debts are the only way most of us can afford to buy expensive things. If it was not for your mortgage, would you be able to purchase a house? Debts help us achieve our personal goals and live the life we want. If you can manage it well, debts can become your greatest asset. Debt is inevitable, which is why learning to stay on top of it is essential to reap maximum benefits from it. It becomes bad the moment it gets out of your control. Understanding and differentiating between the good and the bad is an essential first step of debt management.

Good Debts

There is an old saying that states "It takes money to make money." So if you don't have money, does that mean you will never be able to become wealthy? The American Dream is all about achieving everything that you deserve by putting in your best effort; this is where good debt figures in. It is the debt that helps you achieve your dreams, builds net worth, and helps realize an overall financial upgrade. Some examples of good debts are:

- Education or student debt: Enhancing your knowledge is the greatest gift that you can give yourself. Investing in your education and taking out a loan for the same is good debt because it will help you increase your earning potential. The more educated you are, the higher your chances are of getting a well-paying job. Your student loan will pay for itself in a few years because with a specialized or technical degree, you won't have any trouble in finding your desired jobs. Consider the long-term prospects of the degree you are applying for and ensure that you will be able to repay the loan by analyzing expected earnings.

- Money borrowed to start your business: Taking charge of your career and starting an independent venture can be rewarding and financially viable. When you borrow money for this purpose, it can be classified as good debt because you are taking steps to improve yourself professionally. If you choose a field that you are knowledgeable and passionate about, it hopefully lowers its chances of failure and you can comfortably repay the loan.

- Mortgage or other real estate loan: Investing in a place to live is always a good idea which is why your mortgage is good debt. A house is the biggest asset that you can own and if you plan your finances properly, you might even be able to repay the mortgage before its tenure. Taking out a loan to invest in real estate, whether it is your own home, or an investment property can be classed as good debt.

Bad Debts

A traditional view states that all debts are essentially bad. However, financial experts have come to the conclusion that money borrowed to buy rapidly-depreciating assets or consumer goods can be classified as bad debts. Here are a few examples:

- Car loans: Although it might seem impossible to live without a car, borrowing money to purchase a car is not one of the brightest ideas from a financial perspective because of its high rate of depreciation. If you cannot afford to buy a car outright, try to opt for a loan with low or no interest.
- Consumables and clothes: If you take out a personal loan for buying clothes or other consumables, then it is bad debt. You cannot be in dire need of a leather purse, and especially not enough for you to borrow money for it.
- Credit card and payday loans: Unnecessary spending on your credit card is the ultimate example of bad debt and you must avoid it at all costs because you have to pay interest at a very high rate on these dues. Don't use a credit card unless absolutely necessary. Payday loans are short-term financing options to help you get through a crisis. You have to write a post-dated check and repay the remaining loan when your next paycheck arrives. These loans carry high interest rates and you must not opt for them.

Special Considerations

Like most things in life, debts also have a grey area that cannot be classified as good or bad. Depending on your financial situation, certain debts which are generally classified as bad might end up being good for you. Consider the following examples:

- If you are struggling with a lot of debt, then a debt consolidation loan might be a good option if you can ensure that you use the cash to pay off your debts. This might seem like a loop because it implies debt to cover debt, but it can be an efficient way to manage your finances.

- Many experienced investors with access to a margin account borrow money from their brokers to invest in the share market. For someone who has no clue about investments, this might seem like an absurd idea. However, confident investors who know they will earn money on their investments often opt for such loans.
- If you do not have access to medical insurance, you might need to borrow money in case of a medical emergency. Since you don't have any control over such situations, these debts are often unavoidable. However, most medical debts don't have an interest rate so it won't eat up your savings.

How Much Is Too Much?

Debt is highly relative. Most financially stable people had to borrow money at some point in their lives. You don't have to be scared of it if you have the skills to manage it. However, there is a certain limit that is considered as "too much" by credit experts and financial institutions.

To understand whether you have too many debts, you have to calculate your debt-to-income (DTI) ratio. The formula for DTI is:

DTI = Total Monthly Debt Payments/Gross Monthly Income

For example, let's say you are paying a mortgage of $1,100 every month, credit card bills of $500, and a car loan installment of $200. Your gross monthly pay before taxes is $6,000. So your DTI will be (1,100+500+200)/6,000 = 0.30 or 30%.

This ratio indicates what percentage of your gross income is spent on debts every month. A high DTI might make you ineligible for new lines of credit or you might find it difficult to repay your existing loans. If your DTI is below 36%, your debt is manageable. A DTI higher than 43% is very bad for credit and if it goes above 50% then you might consider options like debt consolidation or even filing for bankruptcy.

CONSOLIDATE DEBTS IF THINGS HAVE GONE OUT OF CONTROL

I know after looking at the formula above you are making a mental calculation of what your DTI is. If the results are freaking you out, then take a deep breath because you have an option to improve your situation. When your debts have gone out of control and you feel like it is almost impossible for you to repay them, consider debt consolidation. Debt consolidation combines all your debts into a larger loan. The aim of this bigger loan is to make things easier for you so it has lower interest rates and the terms of the loan will be favorable for you. The monthly repayments will also be lower. Don't be under the impression that your debts are going away. They are simply being reorganized so that you can repay them without facing any major financial difficulties. Debt consolidation is usually done to combine high-interest debts like credit card dues. It can also be used to consolidate student debt and other liabilities.

Methods of Consolidation

There are two primary methods of debt consolidation:

Balance Transfer Credit Card

In this method, your entire debt will be transferred to a credit card containing a 0% promotional interest rate for a set period of time. If you have a good credit score (greater than 690), you will be able to pay the balance in full during the 0% promotional period. The terms are usually flexible and there is no prepayment penalty. However, it hampers your credit score because of the high use of credit, and in case you are unable to repay during the promotional offer period, your entire debt will attract a high rate of interest. This method should only be used if you have the control and discipline to pay down the debt in the period of time given. The last thing you want is to start accumulating more credit card debt.

Debt Consolidation Loan

These loans are suitable for people who have multiple high-interest loans like credit card debts. The entire debt is transferred to a single loan. You use the money received from the consolidation loan to repay your other debts and pay back the consolidation loan eventually in smaller installments. You don't need to have good credit to be eligible for this loan but if you have a good score then your interest rates will be lower. This is one of the most popular methods of consolidating debt because of its flexibility and easy access.

Apart from these two, there are other options where you need to provide collateral security to obtain a consolidation loan. An example of this type of loan is a home equity line of credit (HELOC) where you use the equity of your house to get a revolving credit line or an installment loan. However, this will affect your credit score. You can also take a loan against your 401(k) plan or consult a credit counselor to set up a debt management plan for you. You must not use your secured debt to replace your unsecured debt because, in case of a default, you might lose your asset.

When Should You Consider Debt Consolidation?

Unfortunately, finding yourself in financial difficulty at some point of your life is quite common. However, you should not think about debt consolidation every time you find your debts overwhelming. Debt consolidation might affect your credit and is a major financial decision which is why you should consider it only under the following circumstances:

- Your DTI is less than 50%. If your monthly debt repayments constitute more than half of your gross monthly income, then debt consolidation is not a good idea for you because you are struggling with your existing debts. There is no way you will be able to repay a debt consolidation loan with such a high DTI.
- You have a good credit score. When your credit score is high you will be eligible for a 0% credit card or a debt consolidation loan at a lower interest rate.
- You have a steady cash flow to service the repayments.
- You will be able to repay a debt consolidation loan within five years.

STRATEGIES TO REDUCE DEBT

Debt consolidation should not be the first thing on your mind when you think about debt management. Ideally you should be thinking about strategies to reduce your debt so that you can fulfill all your financial goals. These methods will provide some guidance on how you can effectively reduce your debt over time:

Highest Interest Rate or Avalanche Method

This method prioritizes repaying the loans that carry the highest interest rates. The strategy would be to make minimum payments on all your loans except for the most expensive ones so that you can utilize the extra money to repay your highest-interest debts. Once you are done with it, it would be time to move on to the next expensive one. This method will save you a lot of time and money because you are repaying the one with the highest interest rate at first. However, it is difficult to make progress with this method if you are not disciplined and committed to the process. Since you will be paying the most expensive debt first, you need to have a steady cash flow which makes it unsuitable for people who have varying incomes throughout the year.

Debt Snowball Method

In this method, the loan with the lowest interest rate is targeted first. The process is similar to that of the debt avalanche method. Here you will be making minimum payments for all your debts except the least expensive one. The philosophy behind this method is to tackle the easier and smaller debts first before moving on to the larger and more expensive ones. Once you have paid off the first debt completely, you can move on to the next one, thereby creating a 'snowball' of debt payments. The biggest reason why this method is popular is that it builds motivation and is easy to implement. Since the smaller debts are repaid faster, you will feel like you are making some actual progress in your debt management process. However, since you will be getting to the more expensive debts last, you will end up paying more interest. This makes this method expensive and it will take you a very long time before you can be completely debt-free.

It is important to note that both these methods apply only to consumer debt and you must never try them for mortgages. If you are applying any of these methods for credit card debt, make sure you are not using the credit card anymore. If you keep purchasing stuff with the card, there would be no point in applying any of these methods.

UNDERSTANDING YOUR CREDIT SCORE

Most of us know the term "credit score" but we don't understand what it means. It is a commonly known fact that if your credit score is bad, then it's difficult to get loans. So we can say that your credit score is a numerical figure calculated by considering various factors which act as proof of your creditworthiness. It is denoted by a number between 300 to 800 and a higher score will improve your eligibility to obtain loans. To manage your debts efficiently, you need to have a good credit score.

When you apply for a loan, a financial institution will conduct an inquiry to find out your credit score. This is known as a "hard inquiry." It is a request to check your credit by a bank or your creditors. This type of inquiry can take up to five points off your FICO score. It will need your consent and will remain on your credit report for about two years, although it will stop affecting it after one year. If you are applying for a prequalification, it will not happen since you only want to find out your eligibility. On the other hand, a "soft inquiry" may be conducted by you to find out your credit score. Credit searches conducted by potential employers, credit card companies calling you to sell their cards, or mortgage brokers also count as soft inquiries. This type of inquiry does not affect your credit score. Some searches can be soft or hard like when you apply to rent an apartment or open a bank account which is why it is better to ask beforehand so that your credit card doesn't get hampered. Understanding your credit score is very important to manage your debts properly.

Getting rid of debts is difficult and often you have to be creative with your strategies. No matter how hard you try to reduce your debts and maintain a credit score, it is difficult to do so with a limited income. You can prepare budgets, set financial goals, and do everything right but your debts will still come and haunt you at night which is why you have to start thinking about ways to make more money.

WORKSHEET: IDENTIFY AND MAKE A PLAN

When preparing your budget you identified all your debts. Now with the help of this worksheet, you will list all the debts you have and refer to your budget to figure out where you can put more money for faster repayments.

Type of Debt	Monthly Repayment	Rate of Interest	Due Date of Payment

According to your financial position and preference, select the snowball method or avalanche method. Then you can use the following template to calculate the repayments:

	Debt 1	Debt 2	Debt 3
Original loan Amount			
Interest rate			
Minimum payment			
Snowball budget			

To determine the amount to be repaid, use the following tables:

	Payment no.	Minimum payment	Additional payment	Snowball roll
Debt 1	1			
	2			
	3			

	Principal	Interest	Balance	Surplus
Debt 1				

6

STEP 4—ACCELERATE YOUR RESULTS

If you don't value your time, neither will others. Stop giving away your time and talents. Value what you know and start charging for it. –Kim Garst

My cousin Sean is an accountant at a medium-sized company. He makes decent money but he already has paid off his mortgage, owns two cars, has a sizable investment portfolio, and regularly goes on foreign vacations. He is around 40. You must be wondering, *How does an accountant have so much money to afford all of this?* I was confused as well until I discovered that he had multiple jobs. He always had a flair for writing which he has now utilized by taking up a job as a freelance writer at a finance magazine. He also provides consultancy services to small shops in his neighborhood that cannot afford a professional financial consultant. He helps them out with their accounting, billing, and other related services. He doesn't charge as much as a qualified professional but a standard fee which is affordable to the shop-owners and beneficial to him as well.

The secret behind his affluent lifestyle is not a single-high paying job, but many side hustles. You might not be an engineer, lawyer, or certified public accountant but that doesn't mean you can't make more money. You have to find ways to maximize your earnings in your current situation so that you can accelerate your financial management journey.

THE FIRE MOVEMENT

Before we start talking about side hustles, we must also look for ways to increase our savings from our current budget. A penny saved is a penny earned, which is why maximizing savings is one of the smartest ways to reach your financial goals. The FIRE movement introduced in the book *Your Money or Your Life* by Vicki Robin and Joe Dominguez was born out of a similar principle. FIRE is an acronym for Financial Independence Retire Early which is based on the principle of extreme savings that would allow you to retire much earlier. It is a plan to save and invest aggressively so that you can retire by your 30s or 40s.

Millennials are constantly searching for meaning in their lives. They want to do something more than the regular 9-to-6 job and follow their passion which is why the FIRE movement has gained popularity among this generation. If you are a follower, you'll have to save around 70% of your income and your target would be to save 30 times your yearly expenses, which would be around $1 million. Once you have saved this much, you can leave your job, start a passion project or quit working completely. After retirement, you can withdraw small amounts (around 3% to 4%) from your savings yearly to cover your living expenses. However, this would require diligence and continuous monitoring so that you can ensure that the expenses are being met justifiably.

Saving 70% of your income might seem impossible, but it is more achievable than you think. Saving extra becomes possible when you look for ways to increase your income. When you are a follower of the FIRE movement, you have to understand that financial independence means not having to work anymore, not just enjoying vacations. The power lies with you because you have the choice of not working.

I once bought all the ingredients for making a Huntsman Pie but the recipe was so difficult I couldn't do it. I ended up using the ingredients for other dishes. If you find the FIRE philosophy difficult, I would suggest that you don't discard it completely. Try to learn the deeper significance of it, even if you cannot follow through. Here are a few things I feel are worth learning from the FIRE movement:

- Think about retirement in a properly planned way. Retirement age doesn't need to be 65 if you have the resources to support yourself.
- There is always a way to cut back on expenses. Even if you can't save 70%, you can try saving more than what you usually do.
- Saving and investing are the top priorities to lead a comfortable life post-retirement.

This becomes possible only when you believe you can do it, so your attitude is very important when it comes to implementing the FIRE movement in your life.

NEGOTIATE FOR A RAISE

Most people working in a full-time job are unhappy with it because they feel like they are not adequately compensated. You are not wrong in thinking that you deserve to be paid more. At the end of the day, money is the most important thing about your job.

Switching to better-paying jobs is advisable, but to become successful in any profession, you have to learn the art of negotiating for a raise. When you work for a long time in a company, it reflects well on your character and even your credit, which is why if you have a stable job you must try to retain it for as long as possible. Staying in a company long-term will only be possible if your salary is increased periodically.

When Is the Right Time?

Timing is the most crucial factor while negotiating a raise. You cannot join a job and ask for a raise the next day. You have to be working there for at least six months or preferably a year before you think about negotiating. You also have to make sure that you are productive and contribute actively to the organization or have taken up some new responsibility voluntarily. You cannot be lazy like Garfield and expect your company to pay you more. Moreover, you have to consider the financial position of the company itself before you ask your boss for a raise. If there is a performance evaluation coming up, it might not be the best time for negotiating.

Some Tips to Help You

You might not feel comfortable going up to your boss and asking for a raise. However, if you want to improve your financial situation, you have to step up your game. Think of all those motivational posters you find in the gym that say things like "Step out of your comfort zone to make big things happen" and let them inspire you to take action. Here are a few tips to help you negotiate better:

Know Your Numbers Correctly

The average base salary of a salesperson is around $60,000 in the US (Indeed, 2021). If you are a salesperson negotiating for a raise, you have to know this figure so that you know that you are asking for a justified amount. Your knowledge will show your employer that you have done your homework before asking for a raise and your chances will be better. Think about a range and stay flexible within it. You cannot ask your boss for a specific amount and suggesting a range makes your employer feel like they are in control.

Reflect on Your Performance

Before you go up to your boss, take some time and reflect on how you have been doing in this role. If there are many others on your professional level, ask yourself if there is something that sets you apart. If you can convince your employer that you are efficient in your job and better than the others, asking for a raise will become easier.

Know the Company Well

Despite working in a company for several years, many employees have no clue about the financial health of a company. Financials are not just limited to the accountants, you can check them out as well irrespective of your department. Before you ask for a raise, research how the company is doing and what the company policy is regarding raises. Make your case strong by having sound knowledge of your company.

Practice Before You Go to Your Boss

You might be a very good speaker but negotiating for a raise is bound to make you nervous which is why you must practice your pitch multiple times before presenting. Ask your friend or partner to provide feedback so that you understand how someone else is feeling after hearing you talk. You must know your boss very well so don't say anything that might offend them. You need them to be on your side while giving the presentation.

Set the Meeting Carefully

Your meeting should be set after careful consideration of the date and time. It should preferably be on a Tuesday or Wednesday because they are the most productive days of the week. Your boss will be busy with other important stuff on Monday and Thursday, and after that the weekend fever sets in which is why it is unsuitable for such conversations. Try to have the meeting around 10:00 a.m. or 11:00 a.m. because your boss will likely be in a good mood after having their morning coffee and dealing with pressing issues earlier.

What If Your Boss Says Yes?

We are always so prepared for bad things to happen to us that we freak out a little when something good happens. If you asked your employer for a pay raise and they said yes, you must be prepared to respond to it appropriately. Don't start doing a happy dance in front of them—keep your composure. When they say yes, don't agree immediately and start with a higher figure than your desired salary. You must be willing to stay flexible in case your boss bargains too much about the amount of hike. Your boss should not feel like you are trying to exploit them which is why you must not give out any wrong vibes. Many times employers will try to dodge you by saying, "Yes, but not right now." In such a case, ask for a specific timeline and try to get confirmation from your boss of when you can expect to get the raise.

How to Handle Rejection

Let's face it, if you go up to your boss and ask for a raise, chances are high that they will refuse. In such a case, you cannot lose your calm and have an outburst. Just because they didn't give you a raise does not mean that you need to quit immediately. Don't make it unnecessarily awkward and instead, try to handle the rejection with an appropriate reaction. Your employer might have their hands tied which is why they cannot approve a raise right now. You can ask them for any other alternative benefits if they seem convinced that you deserve a raise. If they were not on the same page when you delivered your pitch, you can politely ask for feedback as to why they feel differently. Finally, before you conclude the conversation, thank them for their time and leave gracefully. There is no need to apologize because you did not make a mistake when you asked for the raise.

Making the best out of your existing job is always advisable over looking for a new one since you have gained experience and already understand how the company works.

ESTABLISH A SIDE HUSTLE

If you ever asked my Grandpa, he would have told you that working two jobs is something poor people do because they cannot earn enough from one job. Their mentality was different back then and so was the economy. Working two jobs is not a matter of shame; in fact, it is the most sensible thing to do given the current socio-economic situation. After the Covid-19 pandemic, many people started working freelance jobs due to pay cuts or loss of employment. Establishing a side hustle is slowly becoming a necessity if you want to keep up a certain lifestyle.

Choosing the Correct Job

The first basic principle when choosing a side hustle is to consider your skills and passion. For example, my friend Nate is an engineer but he has been playing the guitar since he was a teenager. He was good but he never thought about pursuing music as his full-time career. During the pandemic he had a lot of free time and he started giving online guitar lessons to kids. Now he is making good money from it and even considering buying some professional equipment to enhance the quality of his teaching.

To establish a side hustle, you have to analyze the things you are good at. If you feel that you do not have any specific skills that could be marketable, don't worry. There is something for everyone, which is why I have listed the following things that you can try:

- Teaching, consulting, and training: Consider the examples of Sean and Nate. If you have been working in a certain professional field for a long time, you are bound to have some practical experience. That is why teaching and consultancy are very good options for a side hustle. Social media platforms are very useful when it comes to marketing your services since those posts will easily reach many people. If you have experience with fitness training, you can also provide personal training services to people.
- Manual work: If you are handy, you can opt for manual work as a side hustle. This can include plumbing and electronic work. In case you are artistic, you can also create quirky jewelry or other artsy items and start a small business for them.

- Pet services: Most Americans have pets and they want reliable people to look after their fur babies while they are out. If you have pets or have experience in dealing with pets, providing pet sitting and grooming services can be a very good idea for a side hustle.
- Driving services: Uber and Lyft are constantly hiring new people and you can easily make money at your convenience by exploring such opportunities. You can also take up a job as a delivery executive for UberEats, Postmates, Seamless, or Grubhub.
- Monetize your unused assets: Selling your old and unused items on eBay or Craigslist is a good way to earn extra money. You can open an online thrift store for all those clothes you never used or wore only once. If you have a spare room in your house, you can list that on Airbnb and become a host.

Understanding the Gig Economy

The gig economy is based on temporary, flexible jobs carried out by independent contractors and freelancers. Many sides hustle like part-time teaching jobs or renting out rooms to Airbnb are a part of the gig economy. Since many people work temporary or freelance jobs in a gig economy, it results in an abundance of high-quality and cheap skilled labor. The sharing of skills and resources is one of the main characteristics of the gig economy which is why Uber, Lyft, and Airbnb are the biggest players. After the pandemic hit the world, the gig economy saw a boom because many employers were unable to retain full-time employees and many people started looking for freelance jobs.

Upwork and Fiverr are two platforms that link employers with suitable candidates for freelance jobs. These websites allow free-lance workers to respond to job listings for individual and ongoing assignments. On Upwork, you have to create your portfolio by listing your experience, qualifications, skills, and hourly rate. The worker has to respond to the jobs set by the employer. On Fiverr, the candidate has the choice of listing their gig. A client can submit an order based on their requirements and then you will need to complete it accordingly.

The gig economy has facilitated the development of side hustles to a great extent. The best part about most of these side hustles is that you don't need to make any major investments to get started. Once you find your ideal job, you can jump right in. The extra money that you earn will help you save more and once you have achieved your savings goals, you can start thinking about developing an investment strategy.

WORKSHEET: FIND YOUR IDEAL SIDE HUSTLE

Looking for the ideal side hustle can be a challenge since there are so many options. This worksheet will help you figure out which jobs are ideal for you.

First, prepare this list of past jobs you have had and any associated education.

Past Job	Number of Years of Experience	Relevant Educational/ Technical Training for the Job

Once you have made this list, let's look at the following table:

Name of the Job	Your Performance/ Significant Successes	How Much Does This Job Excite You? (Write a few lines and give a rating out of 10.)

Once you have identified the jobs you enjoy the most, you can think about selecting that as a side hustle.

7

STEP 5—DEVELOP AN INVESTMENT PLAN

How many millionaires do you know who have become wealthy by investing in savings accounts? I rest my case. –Robert G. Allen

Jennifer is very serious about saving money. She is cautious and never goes over her budget. She has automated her savings, which means that every week, a portion of her paycheck is deposited into a savings account. She's been working for more than five years and she has a good amount of money in her bank. Yet, you wouldn't be able to call her rich because her wealth is nowhere near what it should be. She learned everything about saving money but skipped the part where you have to invest if you want your money to grow. Keeping money in a savings account is similar to keeping it inside a piggy bank: The money will simply be set aside and you won't be able to reap benefits from it.

Savings is the first step of money management. Unless you learn to save, you won't have a financial backup. However, the investment must be your priority if you wish to achieve financial independence. Savings alone will get you nowhere, you need to find a way to grow your money exponentially. There is no point in being scared of investments because once you understand how it works, there is no going back.

MAKING AN INVESTMENT PLAN

For someone completely new to managing their finances, investing might seem intimidating. Most people fear that if they invest their money, they might lose it. There are also many financial 'sharks' out there who are very willing to take your money. I won't disregard your fears because many people have incurred losses after investing but if you have the right knowledge and attitude, you won't. Investing money is an essential part of growing your wealth, which is why it is important to learn about. I would strongly recommend that you do your research (thoroughly) and understand the asset class that you intend to invest in. It is your hard earned money so it's important to make good, informed decisions and with the help of an organized investment plan, you will be able to achieve your financial goals.

Step 1: Analyze Your Current Situation

The biggest mistake people make is that they start investing without considering the related factors. Just because your friend bought a mutual fund, doesn't mean you have to do it as well. The first important step before you start investing is to consider your financial situation. Take out that budget you prepared in Chapter 3. If you feel like your cash flow is comfortable and you have enough money in your hands to start investing, then consider the amount you can spare for that purpose. Consider the liquidity of the investments. If you frequently need cash, you might want to opt for an option from where funds can be easily withdrawn.

Step 2: Define Your Goals

The previous chapters must have given you an idea of what your financial goals look like. Now is the time to start thinking about a timeline for when you wish to achieve those goals. Your goals can be classified according to the following categories:

- Safety: Maintaining your current level of wealth is an objective for most people.
- Income: How much are you looking to earn from your investments? Do you wish to earn a quick profit?
- Growth: You might want to sit back and watch your wealth grow.

Step 3: Consider Your Risk Appetite

The general notion is that if you are young, you must be willing to take risks since you have a lot more time to recover from any potential losses. However, you might have a lower risk appetite and there is no need to shame yourself for that. Everyone is different and you must not do anything that makes you extremely uncomfortable. Some people have a naturally high risk-tolerance level. If that doesn't sound like you, explore the options gradually because the more you know, the less scared you will be. Older people must consider relatively safer options because they might not be able to earn back the losses.

Step 4: Decide Where to Invest

Your goals and risk appetite will determine what kind of an investor you are. If you want a quick profit, you might want to be more active in managing your portfolio than someone who simply wants their wealth to grow. Beware of any get rich quick schemes –

invariably this will not have a happy ending. This chapter will focus on the various investment options available to you as per your requirement – most of what is covered is a get rich slow approach. Being aware of all your options will help you create a diverse portfolio so that you don't lose your money even if the market takes a downward turn.

UNDERSTANDING ASSET CLASSES AND TYPES OF INVESTMENT OPTIONS

Investment analysts have created bundles of assets based on their behavior in the financial market and the rules and regulations that they are subject to. Such similar groups of assets are called asset classes. The three main asset classes are equities or stocks, fixed-income instruments or bonds, and cash equivalent or money market instruments. In today's dynamic economy, it is best to have a diverse portfolio with different asset classes so that you can reduce the risk. Most professional investors like to have a mix of stocks, mutual funds, real estate, commodities, derivatives, and cryptocurrencies to fetch optimum returns.

To ensure that you do not make any mistake in your investment strategy, you have to understand each of the following elements very thoroughly.

Stocks/Equities

When you buy the stocks of a public company, you are essentially subscribing to a part of their capital and becoming the owner of that part of the company. Investing in stocks gives the investor maximum benefit if they can hold the investment for a long time. Stocks can be very volatile which is why many people are scared to invest in them. You have to remain patient and hope that the company will be able to provide you with a profit. Since the market is filled with stocks of multiple companies, you have to conduct thorough research before buying an individual stock.

There are usually two main types of stocks: Common and preferred. Common stock is what the name suggests—a common instrument that allows you to own a part of the company. You get voting rights and dividends if the company is doing well or has the policy to distribute dividends. Common stock is good for a beginner and you can earn a lot of money when the value of the stock appreciates. Preferred stock pays fixed dividends and usually does not have any other rights. It is good if you are looking for regular income but unsuitable for long-term growth.

Bonds

Bonds are financial instruments that acknowledge a loan given by you to a company or the government. You will receive interest at a fixed rate from the borrower who will use your funds for their business purpose. Bonds have a low rate of return, typically around 5% in comparison to stocks, which fetch much higher average long-term returns of 10%. A bond is a safe investment because you will never lose your money which is why it is a good addition to your portfolio to balance the risk associated with investing in stocks. Bonds are of the following types:

- US Treasury Bonds: Backed up by the Federal Government, these bonds are your safest investment but they provide the lowest returns. Common types of treasury bonds are bills and notes.
- Corporate Bonds: When a company requires financing to expand their operations, they might issue corporate bonds to the public at a specified interest rate. Buying corporate bonds of a company does not make you an owner of the company, it makes you a creditor. Most

corporate bonds come with a credit rating. A high credit rating indicates that the bond is of investment-grade and has a lower chance of default. Bonds of public sector companies have a good rating, but the return is lower. A low credit rating will indicate a higher chance of default but the rate of return can be very high on such bonds. A new startup might not have a good credit rating, but if they perform very well and earn profits their bonds have the capacity to fetch high rates of return.

- Municipal Bonds: Also known as munis, these bonds are issued by local or state governments, counties, or other non-federal government entities. They fund city and state projects like building schools or hospitals and provide tax benefits to the holder. They may be short-term and repaid within three years, or long-term and repaid within approximately 10 years.

If your investment portfolio primarily consists of stocks, you might want to add some bonds to it because it is a safe investment option generating a fixed income at a regular frequency. However, many people don't prefer it due to the low interest rates. Bonds are risky in a different sense because the interest rates might suddenly go up and then you won't be able to sell it. For example, you have a bond that gives you 5% interest p.a. Now, the interest rates have gone up and other bonds are fetching 5.5% p.a. In such a situation, nobody will want to buy a low-paying bond because there are better options available.

Cash and Cash Equivalents

The money that you are setting aside in your savings account or fixed deposits is also a form of investment. They provide a low return on investment but are safe investments because you will never lose your money from these modes.

Commodities

Mostly suitable for highly-experienced investors, commodities include agricultural products, energy products and metals, and other raw materials used by the industry. They are high-risk investments as prices can fluctuate depending on the demand and market supply. In case you are wondering, you won't be buying 'physical' commodities; rather, the investment takes place through futures and options. Trading is done using derivative instruments which is why you need to know the same before investing in them.

Mutual Funds and Exchange Traded Funds (ETFs)

Mutual Funds and ETFs are financial instruments that invest in a variety of stocks, bonds, and commodities according to a specific strategy. It is ideal for the first-time investor because when you buy units of a mutual fund, you are automatically investing in a balanced portfolio of diverse funds.

I personally like EFTs. ETFs were mostly passively managed, as they typically track a market index or sector sub-index, e.g. they might invest in 80-100 American companies across a broad range of industries with an emphasis on identifying quality companies. This helps to spread the investment risk and minimize expose to a small number of companies or sectors. Always check the fees, they should be lower than mutual funds.

Having a clear knowledge of all types of investment options will give you clarity as to which one is most suitable for you.

COMPOUNDING INTEREST AND HOW IT HELPS YOUR MONEY GROW

When I say investments have the potential to grow your money exponentially, what exactly does it mean? Why do investments grow at a higher rate than your typical savings account? The answer is compound interest.

You might have learned about compound interest back in school, but I'm not sure how much of it has stuck with you. Let's refresh our memory. Compounding interest calculates interest on both the principal which you initially deposited and interest that you earned. It means that you are earning interest on interest which makes money grow at a faster rate than simple interest. The amount of interest accrual will depend on the frequency of compounding. The formula for compound interest is as follows:

$$= [P\,(1 + i)^n] - P$$
$$= P\,[(1 + i)^n - 1]$$

(please stick with me as it gets really interesting...)

Where P = principal, i = nominal annual interest rate in percentage terms, and n = number of compounding periods. Let us understand this with a numerical example to make it simpler.

Suppose you have an initial amount of $2,000 at an interest rate of 5% that compounds annually. In the first year, you will earn 5% of $2,000 = $100 which would bring your total balance to $2,000+$100 = $2,100. Next year your interest will be calculated on the total balance of $2,100, which would come to $105 and be added to the total balance, making it $2,205. This process will keep going till the maturity of your investment. Simple interest will only consider the initial principal amount, which means your interest will be $100 every year till maturity. The more frequently your money compounds, the greater your money will grow. If you find this math confusing, don't worry because numerous online calculators will help you to calculate the returns easily. However, you must understand the logic behind the calculation. Simple interest is often used to calculate interest on car loans or other short-term loans while mortgages, student loans, personal loans, and credit card debts compound their interest.

Here is another example of the beauty of compound interest. You start a part time job at 15 and manage to scrape together $5000 a year and invest in a low cost EFT fund and reinvest any dividends paid out. Along the way you earn 10% and then you stop at the age of 24. Your friend starts later than you, at age 25 but keeps investing until he is 60. Who will have the most money at age 60?

Age	You invest	Compounding	Your friend invests	Compounding
15	5000	5,500		
16	5000	11,550		
17	5000	18,205		
18	5000	25,526		
19	5000	33,578		
20	5000	42,436		
21	5000	52,179		
22	5000	62,897		
23	5000	74,687		
24	5000	87,656		
25		96,421	5000	5,500
26		106,064	5000	11,550
27		116,670	5000	18,205
28		128,337	5000	25,526
29		141,171	5000	33,578
30		155,288	5000	42,436
31		170,816	5000	52,179
32		187,898	5000	62,897
33		206,688	5000	74,687
34		227,357	5000	87,656
35		250,092	5000	101,921
36		275,102	5000	117,614
37		302,612	5000	134,875
38		332,873	5000	153,862
39		366,160	5000	174,749
40		402,776	5000	197,724
41		443,054	5000	222,996
42		487,359	5000	250,795
43		536,095	5000	281,375
44		589,705	5000	315,012
45		648,675	5000	352,014

46		713,543	5000	392,715
47		784,897	5000	437,487
48		863,387	5000	486,735
49		949,725	5000	540,909
50		1,044,698	5000	600,500
51		1,149,167	5000	666,050
52		1,264,084	5000	738,155
53		1,390,493	5000	817,470
54		1,529,542	5000	904,717
55		1,682,496	5000	1,000,689
56		1,850,746	5000	1,106,258
57		2,035,820	5000	1,222,383
58		2,2394,02	5000	1,350,122
59		2,4633,43	5000	1,490,634
60		**2,709,677**	5000	**1,645,197**

Chart taken from The Barefoot Investor, Scott Pape.

When you put your money in savings accounts, certificates of deposit, 401(k) accounts, and other investment accounts, you get the benefit of compounding. Compound interest has the real potential to make you rich as it grows your money exponentially. Mutual funds are another example that reaps maximum benefits from compounding by reinvesting the dividends received.

You have to be patient to reap the benefits of compound interest as it takes time to make your money grow. That is why it is important to start investing money as early as possible so that as you near retirement, your compounded wealth will reach a significant amount.

Real Estate

Real estate is a form of long-term investment and includes buying a piece of land, building, or simply a home to live in. It can be risky depending on the economy, public school rating, and local government stability. If you don't like the idea of managing your property by yourself, you can also purchase Real Estate Investment Trusts (REITs), which are instruments issued by companies that use real estate to make money for their shareholders.

Unlike stock and bond investors, prospective real estate owners can use *leverage* to buy a property by paying a portion of the total cost upfront. In chapter 8, I explore in more detail about home ownership. However, you can decide to invest in property in other ways. Suppose you take out a mortgage and put the house on rent. You ensure that the income received from the property will be enough to repay the monthly installments on the loan. Over the long term, your loan will be repaid and you will be left with the home equity along with the regular income from your property.

Understanding leverage as a tool to build wealth

Leverage is an investment strategy of using borrowed money e.g. a mortgage - to increase the potential return of an investment. For example, I could buy a property for $300,000, put a 20% deposit of my own money and get a mortgage for $240,000. Over time, my rent pays off the mortgage of my rental and I am left with an asset that is debt free and an asset that should have increased. If my asset has doubled in 15 years then my initial investment of $60,000 has turned into a $600,000 asset. What if I bought three properties? That could result in assets worth $1.8 million. This is a simplistic way of looking at this asset class as there will be costs to hold the property over this time, plus the upkeep as well as times when the property will be vacant. But if you do your research (thoroughly) and invest in an area which is primed for growth over the long term, that has low vacancy rates and where the rent covers most of the mortgage repayment then it could be a strategy worth thinking about.

AGE-WISE INVESTING STRATEGIES

Your taste in fashion and romantic partners changes as you grow older (one would hope). Your investment strategy should also change as you age. The things that are safe in your 20s or 30s won't be the same in your 40s or 50s as your retirement age comes near. Your priorities will change and your investment strategy should be created to keep up with them. You will also find that as your confidence grows your investments could become more 'sophisticated'. For example, it might be prudent to place some of your investments in a trust structure. Since most of these recommendations are quite general, I would suggest that you consult a financial advisor who can help you eliminate any chances of making a mistake.

As a general rule of thumb, you must have living expenses of 6 to 12 months saved up in a savings account that can be withdrawn anytime. According to your age group, this can be a recommended investment mix:

- The 20s: The lion's share (around 80 to 90%) of your investment portfolio should consist of stocks to reap the maximum benefits of compound interest. Invest aggressively because your wealth will grow hugely within a decade. The remaining can be invested in bonds and other safe investments.
- The 30s: If your 20s did not allow you to invest aggressively due to the burden of loans, you should start now by putting 70 to 80% of your money in stocks and the remaining in bonds. Now would be the time to match your employer's contribution to the 401(k) and put money in IRAs as well.
- The 40s: You are now at the peak of your career and earning potential which is why you should invest 60 to 70% in stocks, and 30 to 40% in bonds along with maximum contributions to IRA and 401(k).
- The 50s and 60s: As you are nearing the age of retirement, you must consider more stable investment options, which is why your portfolio should consist of 50

to 60% stocks and 40 to 50% bonds. The IRA allows you to put more money in investment accounts as well.

- The 70s and 80s: At this point, you have probably retired or will retire soon. Your portfolio needs to have dividend-paying stocks and most of your money should be invested in bonds. You will be collecting social security benefits at this age as well.

Be proactive

As you delve deeper into the world of investments, you will feel interested to explore more options. Investments have the potential to make you truly wealthy which is why you must try your hand at everything starting from stocks to real estate. Even if you find long-term investments like real estate intimidating, you must think twice before rejecting them because they can look after you in your lifetime and create generational wealth.

WORKSHEET: INVESTMENT STRATEGY

This worksheet will help you figure out your risk appetite and which investment strategy is best for you. Remember that it will change over time, so make sure to refer to it periodically and make necessary changes.

Questions	Your Comments Here
What are your long-term financial goals and return requirements? What kind of return do you need and in what period? (Your return does not need to be a specific percentage, just write and explain what comes to your mind.)	
What risks are you willing to take? (You can only risk something that you can afford to lose.)	
Are there any non-negotiables/constraints with your investing?	
What is your general knowledge about investing in stocks? Do you feel comfortable putting your money in stocks?	
How would you describe yourself in terms of risk tolerance?	
If your savings goal is more than 20 years away, then most of your portfolio should consist of stocks. If you have a shorter goal (e.g. within five years) then you should consider a low-risk portfolio or savings account.	

8

STEP 6—EXPLORE BECOMING A HOMEOWNER

"I will forever believe that buying a home is a great investment. Why?
Because you can't live in a stock certificate. You can't live in a mutual fund."
–Oprah Winfrey

A lot of us are often very confused about what our priorities should be. Many of my friends who own expensive jewelry, designer handbags, and fancy cars do not have any investments. They live in rented apartments and pay a huge credit card bill every month. I am sure if they cut back a little, they would be able to afford a lot of other important things like real estate or stocks. When I first moved to New York, I used to live in the suburbs because I couldn't afford a place in the city. I lived in a rented apartment with two other friends and we were all looking for a property to purchase. We searched for houses within the neighborhood we were living in but I soon realized that those properties were way out of my budget. So I did some research and bought a place located in a far more interior neighborhood. My friends did not like the location and continued looking for houses near where we lived. Within a few years, the entire neighborhood developed and real estate prices surged higher. The search for the "perfect property" made my friends lose out because they could no longer afford property even in the interiors.

People are often very emotional when it comes to purchasing real estate. I saw that house in the interiors as an investment that would fetch me income and security after retirement. I knew that over time the area would develop and my returns would increase because I bought the property at a cheaper rate. Buying a home is the best investment you can make because its value appreciates over time. The structure of the house might depreciate but the value of the land will still increase. Many small American towns have seen huge economic development in the last two decades. As a neighborhood develops, new amenities come into the picture, which in turn increases the value of the place and your property. Since ancient times, owning land has been a sign of prosperity because only the kings and the nobles could afford it. The famous author Mark Twain said, "Buy land, they are not making it anymore." I like this statement not because it is inspirational but because it is so relevant. The entire world is seeing a crisis in real estate due to an increase in population, which is why you must consider investing in it. This chapter will help you remove any confusion regarding real estate investment so that you can make a well-informed decision.

HOME EQUITY AND HIGH UPFRONT COSTS—TWO FACTORS BEHIND HOMEOWNERSHIP

Real estate stands apart from all other modes of investment because of one unique feature known as home equity. Home equity, as briefly explained in the previous chapter, is the value of the homeowner's interest in their home. For example, if the value of the house is $250,000 and you have taken a loan for $200,000 to purchase the house, the value of home equity for you will be

$50,000. It is the real market value of the property reduced by any loan you have on the property. If you buy a house by taking out a mortgage, the bank or financial institution that has given you the loan will have an interest on your property to the extent of the amount advanced by them. Home equity is that portion of the home's current value that you will own. This might not make much sense to you because all that comes to your mind when you think about real estate investment is a mortgage and how you have to repay it every month. Consider this: As you keep repaying the loan, the bank's interest reduces and your ownership increases. By the time you have repaid your mortgage, the value of your property has increased significantly and now you are the owner of an asset which you bought for a much lesser price. You can even get credit against your home equity which, as mentioned in Chapter 5, is called the HELOC.

You might be getting the impression that homeownership is a smooth ride and filled with unique advantages. While this is undoubtedly true, you must also consider that there are some peculiarities as well. You must be aware of all the nuances before you commit yourself to an investment.

There is a reason why homeownership is considered to be the investment of the wealthy and middle class. You might be thinking that if you are taking out a mortgage, the down payment is the only amount that you will pay—but there is more to it than that. Apart from the down payment, there are certain other closing costs that you have to incur, including an application fee, appraisal fee, attorney's fee, property taxes, mortgage insurance, home inspection, homeowner's insurance premium, title insurance, title search, points (prepaid insurance), origination fee, recording fee, and survey fee (Probasco, 2019). All these fees might add up to a lot of money thereby increasing the initial investment required to purchase real estate.

RENTING VS HOMEOWNERSHIP

According to a 2019 Survey of Consumer Finances, the median homeowner has 40 times the wealth of a renter (Kushi, 2020). However, this is not the only index you should look at when deciding whether you should buy or rent a house. I find making a pros and cons list is always helpful when you have to evaluate two alternatives.

Pros of Homeownership

We have already talked about how home equity is one of the unique benefits of owning real estate. Here are a few other important benefits you will enjoy when you purchase a property:

Great Returns in the Long Run

When you consider investing in real estate, you must discard the idea of making a quick profit because it takes a lot of time and patience to earn good returns. Real estate prices follow a cyclical trend, which means you can often expect heavy downward fluctuations in the price of your property. For example, after the 2008 financial crisis, prices of real estate were at an all-time low. Investors were devastated, but the ones who kept their calm and held on to the investment eventually ended up making profits because prices increased after a while. If you have the funds and you are eligible for a mortgage, buying a house is the best thing you can do because it will give you phenomenal returns in the long run due to appreciation and home equity. Moreover, housing costs become stable after a while so you end up incurring far less after you have purchased the property.

Pride and Community

Owning a house has always been a matter of immense pride for some people. Your position in your community can be strengthened when you become a homeowner. This might not seem like much, but your investment goes beyond a financial transaction. The privacy of your home provides comfort, security, and a sense of accomplishment.

Tax Incentives and Deductions

One of the biggest benefits that real estate investment provides is that of tax incentives. When you sell your property, you won't be liable to pay capital gain taxes if your gain does not exceed $250,000 provided that property was your place of residence for two years in the last five years. Moreover, when you own real estate, you can also claim deductions for the expenses you incur concerning the property from your taxes. This will include your mortgage interest, which can turn out to be thousands of dollars every year.

Cons of Home Ownership

High upfront costs are probably the biggest disadvantage when it comes to real estate investment. However, it is not the only disadvantage. Here are a few major problems associated with buying a property:

Long Term Commitment

Once you buy a property, you need to hold it for a considerable time period before you can reap benefits from it. Such long-term commitment might not be suitable for everyone.

Lack of Flexibility and Liquidity

Real estate investments are not flexible or liquid. If you find yourself in sudden need of cash, real estate will be of no use because selling it takes a lot of time. So if you are someone who often faces cash crunches, real estate investments might not be the best thing for you.

Maintenance and Repair Costs

When you become a homeowner, you become responsible for many other regular expenses other than your mortgage. You have to pay for utilities like electricity, water and sewage, and trash pickup. You have to pay for property taxes, pest control, homeowner's insurance, earthquake or flood insurance, and incur expenses for routine repairs and maintenance.

Moreover, if you are unable to service your mortgage, there is a possibility of foreclosure which means you will end up losing your property.

Pros of Renting a House

For someone who is just looking for a place to live, renting is the best option because it is completely hassle-free. Here are a few benefits that make renting an attractive option:

Lower Costs

Renting is significantly less expensive than owning a house because your obligation is limited to your rent and not destroying the property. There is no headache about a down payment or unexpected closing costs because it is not your liability. You won't have to worry about repairs and maintenance costs as well because they will be taken care of by your landlord.

Flexibility

Your commitment to your rented apartment is limited to your lease period. You can even leave before that provided you give proper notice. Renting an apartment is much more flexible and it is ideal if your employment situation is not yet stable or you have to move around a lot.

Cons of Renting a House

Renting has many disadvantages which are listed as follows:

No Tax Incentives or Deductions

When you pay rent, you do not get any tax incentives because it is simply an expense that you are incurring.

You Are Not Building Any Equity

Despite incurring all those extra expenses, homeownership is associated with building equity. When you rent a house, you do not gain anything from it apart from a place to live. It is not your asset, so there is no question of building equity.

Apart from these disadvantages, you are completely at the mercy of your landlord. After providing reasonable notice, they can ask you to leave anytime and you might not be able to do anything about it. Increasing rent is one of the major problems faced by Americans right now and you may find yourself in the same boat if you choose to rent a house.

Homeownership comes with its perks but you will have significant responsibilities and incur extra expenses as well. The main reason why homeownership is encouraged is that it is a tangible asset that is going to support you throughout your life. All your earnings won't matter if you are unable to support yourself after retirement, which is exactly why you must start preparing now.

WORKSHEET: DETERMINE WHETHER IT'S MORE LUCRATIVE TO RENT VS BUY A HOME

Now is the time to analyze which option is more suitable for you. With the help of this worksheet, you will be able to make an informed decision.

Questions	Your Comments Here
Take a look at your assets. What assets do you own?	
What is the average price of houses in the area that you are interested in? (Write down a number.)	
Determine how much down payment you can make after considering your savings. What percentage of the total amount would this figure be? (Note: Since many costs add up, you must wait if you cannot put down around 20% of the purchase price.)	
Calculate your Debt-to-Income Ratio (DTI): • Front-End DTI: Divide your projected monthly housing expenses (mortgage plus taxes plus insurance) by your monthly gross income. • Back-End DTI: Divide all of your monthly expenses (projected housing, loan, credit card payments) by your monthly gross incomes. [Note: The ideal front-end DTI is below 28% and back-end DTI is below 36%]	
Create your five-year plan: Where do you see yourself in five years? (Note: If you have plans to shift soon, it is better to rent.)	
If you want to buy a home, how long do you want to stay there? (Note: If you have long-term plans to settle with your family, then homeownership is ideal for you.)	
Are you willing to put time and energy into a property?	
What does your job situation look like? (Note: If you don't have a stable job yet, it might be best to wait before buying a house.)	

9

STEP 7—PLAN FOR RETIREMENT

You cannot escape the responsibility of tomorrow by evading it today.
–Abraham Lincoln

Uncle Sam worked as the manager of a small store. Don't confuse the title 'manager' with something glamorous; all he did was supervise a few workers and handle customer complaints. This was his job profile for the last 20 years and he lived a simple life. He retired last year and you would be surprised to see how he's living his life now. No, he's not miserable or in need of money. He is living the best life! He goes for a jog every morning. His Facebook wall is filled with pictures from his travels around the world and it looks like he is finally able to pursue his passion of bird-watching. He bought a professional camera and you won't believe how beautiful the pictures are.

You must be wondering how a person like Uncle Sam, who had a mediocre income all his life, can afford such a lifestyle after retirement. The answer is two words: Retirement planning. Uncle Sam started planning for his retirement very early in his life, which is why despite being in the middle-income bracket all his life, he is leading a financially stable post-retirement life.

For someone who is in their 20s or even 30s, retirement is a distant thought. Nobody likes to think about growing old, but when you find that stray grey hair or suddenly feel pain in your back after waking up, you will get a reality check. I first thought about it when I 'noticed' my parents growing old. My mom was one of the most independent people I knew and one day I saw her asking for help while she was moving a few boxes. I never thought about Mom needing help for anything because she was always like Wonder Woman for us. However, our physical abilities deteriorate significantly as we grow older; it's harder to work as much and even simple things feel more difficult to do, which is why we have to think ahead and make provisions for such inevitabilities when we are young. If you close your eyes to what is inevitable, you will be the one who loses. It is better to stay prepared because, in the end, you will have nobody to blame but yourself. In this chapter we will explore how and where you can put your money *today* to ensure a secure post-retirement life for yourself tomorrow.

PLANNING FOR RETIREMENT

Contrary to what you might feel, talking or thinking about retirement does not make you 'old,' it makes you a responsible adult who knows how to plan your future. Retirement planning is a process that you should start as early as possible so that you have plenty of time later on to make adjustments to the initial plan. Life often takes unpredictable turns which is why you need to be prepared for anything that comes your way. When you decide to start planning for retirement, here are five steps that you must follow to make the process simpler.

Step 1: Know the Right Timeline for Every Goal

Your 20s are the perfect time to start your retirement planning. However, it is never too late and you must not feel discouraged if you haven't started yet. The more time you have until your retirement, the greater the risk component in your investment portfolio will be. You will have multiple short-term and long-term financial goals and you have a specific amount of time available to achieve them. Every time one of your goals is achieved, your portfolio is rebalanced and you have to reassess your portfolio once again to figure out where you stand. When you have more than 30 years left for retirement, you can invest most of your money in riskier stocks, but you have to change the portfolio every few years and transfer funds to more stable instruments. This will ensure that your financial priorities are at par with your age.

Step 2: Determine How Much You Will Need After Retirement

Let's face it, you are not going to become a saint after you retire. It is unrealistic to assume that your lifestyle will drastically change once you stop working. You have gotten used to living a certain way for all these years, so how can you expect yourself to alter all your ways at the age of 60? Unreasonable expectations like these often lead to wrong decisions. Around 70 to 80% of your living expenses is not enough provision for your post-retirement life. You should aim to make a provision of 100% of living expenses in your pre-retirement phase so that you won't have to compromise when it comes to your standard of living. You will finally have enough time to do all the things you could not do during your working days. You can travel, go sightseeing, and tick off all the things on your bucket list once you retire. Moreover, you might need to incur unforeseen expenses like medical bills or your child's education, so you need to be prepared for that.

Step 3: Calculate After-Tax Real Rate of Return

You have defined your goals and allotted a specific period of time to achieve them. You have even created a suitable portfolio according to your age and risk-tolerance level. Despite doing everything right, your returns might get messed up because you considered the incorrect rate of return. Suppose you invested in a bond that gives a 10% return and some stocks that fetch an average return of 15%. When you sell these financial instruments, you expect to get the returns as per the description. However, in reality, the rate that you end up getting is much less than what is mentioned. This is because you forgot to factor in elements like taxes and inflation. For instance, if the inflation for that particular year turned out to be around 2%, that would make your return from bonds 8% and your return from stocks 13%. Because you are selling these instruments at a profit, you will also have to incur capital gains taxes. Your net return will be lower than what you see in the portfolio and that can cause significant trouble in case of large amounts.

Let us understand with a numerical example how after-tax return is usually calculated. Consider the stock portfolio fetching a 15% return and suppose your applicable tax rate is 12%. This would make the after-tax return 15%(1-0.12) = 13.20%. Now if the applicable inflation rate is 2%, the after-tax real rate of return would be $[(1+0.1320)/(1+0.02)]-1 = 10.98\%$. As you can see, this is much less than the rate of return you have earned.

Depending on the type of investment account you hold, you will be taxed for your returns, so it is very important to determine the real after-tax rate of return on your investments.

Step 4: Select Investments According to Your Risk-Tolerance Level

You and your friend Rachel are in your late 20s and have started planning for retirement at the same time. Both of you have done enough research and you know what needs to be done to start the planning process. Rachel has put most of her money in high-risk stocks and is asking you to do the same because that is the right thing to do at your age. However, you are skeptical because you have ailing parents and you feel like you might need to take care of them financially at some point in the future. Moreover, you have certain other personal commitments which require you to keep cash handy at all times. In such a scenario, you must not follow the general rules or give in to peer pressure. Retirement planning should be tailored as per your needs: You should always consider your risk-tolerance level before making any investments because it is your money and you know your requirements better than anyone else. If you feel unsure about putting all your money in risky stocks, then don't do it. Set aside a substantial part of it and invest it in fixed-income securities. The correct risk-return payoff is very important while selecting your retirement investments. There are multiple options available, as discussed in the next section.

Step 5: Estate Planning

I don't want to sound morbid, but you have to ensure that you make proper arrangements regarding what happens to your assets once you are unable to handle them on your own. This doesn't always imply death; you might become mentally or physically incapable of managing your affairs and that is why you have to make a proper plan. An estate plan is a significant part of your retirement planning process and you must start thinking about it as soon as you are acquiring your assets. Don't be under the misconception that estate planning is only for the rich—everyone who owns assets should do it. Usually estate planning includes a life insurance plan, tax planning for the assets you wish to leave as a gift or inheritance, and how expenses will be managed in your absence. An estate plan is very important because it protects the beneficiaries (especially close family members) and saves them from unfavorable situations.

RETIREMENT INVESTMENT PLANS

Most employers are now shifting away from providing traditional pensions. Many people work multiple freelance jobs and none of the employers provide any kind of retirement benefits. Even if your employer has a retirement plan, it is your responsibility to start saving for retirement. According to a survey conducted by the Center for Retirement Research in 2021, nearly 50% of households are "at-risk" for not having enough money to maintain their current standard of living after retirement. If you have never thought about the options available to you, don't worry because I will guide you through all the details in this section.

Individual Retirement Account (IRA)

An IRA is an account which you can use to save money for retirement. It is usually tax deferred or sometimes tax-free. It can be opened by almost anybody and if you use it correctly, you will be able to build a solid retirement fund for yourself. There are two main types of IRAs: Traditional and Roth. Each of these types have multiple variations.

Traditional IRA

This is ideal for anyone who is looking to save for their retirement even if they have access to an employer-sponsored plan like a 401(k) plan. You can have multiple IRAs provided your contributions are limited to the ceiling limit. The contributions are tax-deferred and are not tied to an employer-sponsored plan. Anybody can open an IRA and claim a tax deduction subject to certain conditions. The biggest benefit of a traditional IRA is that it provides a wide investment selection to the investor. However, the contribution limits are lower than a 401(k) plan and tax deductions are phased out at higher income levels. It has a mandatory distribution requirement at age 72 and the distributions are taxed as ordinary income after retirement.

Roth IRA

If you are looking for a retirement investment account, but you won't benefit from contributing to a traditional IRA, you can opt for a Roth IRA. This is suitable for individuals belonging to the middle or lower-income level because deductions to a Roth IRA are made from after-tax dollars and are hence not tax-deductible. Similar to a traditional IRA, a Roth IRA also offers a large investment selection. The other benefits of a Roth IRA are that the qualified withdrawals are tax-free and the contributions can be withdrawn at any time. Moreover, there are no minimum distributions on retirement. However, the problem with Roth IRA is that there are no immediate tax benefits and the contributions are not allowed at higher income levels.

401(k) Plan

A 401(k) plan allows you to choose a certain amount which you can set aside as savings for your retirement. These plans are called defined contribution plans. A 401(k) is an employer-sponsored plan which means you won't have access to one if you are self-employed. If you get a 401(k) plan as a part of your employment package, you can choose to contribute a certain amount subject to the statutory regulations to that account which will remain saved for your retirement. Your employer might also match your contributions to the 401(k) account. This is a very good way for salaried people to create a retirement savings account. The money that you are contributing to this account is invested in safe financial instruments of the stock market so that your income grows and you receive a good sum of money after your retirement. Since they are directly deducted before calculating taxes, 401(k) contributions help reduce your taxable income. After retirement, when you do withdraw the amount from this account, an income tax on such withdrawal will be incurred.

There is a type of Roth 401(k) plan that gives you the option of contributing from your after-tax income which means your taxable income will not be reduced. This makes sense for someone who anticipates they will be in a higher tax bracket after their retirement. The biggest benefit of a 401(k) plan is that you might get a matching employer contribution. Your employer might match your contribution dollar-for-dollar up to 3% of your total salary or they might provide a $0.50 match for every dollar up to a total of 5%. The annual contribution limits for 2020 and 2021 are $19,500. Since the objective of the plan is to save for retirement, the IRS imposes a 10% penalty for any withdrawal before the age of 50.5. Moreover, you will also be subject to a withholding tax of 20% for the amount withdrawn.

The plan is beneficial because your eligibility will not be limited by your income and the contribution limits are pretty high. However, the investment options are limited and you have no control over the cost of the plan. Required minimum distributions begin at age 72.

When you make enough provisions for your retirement, you won't have to depend on your children or anyone else. This will help you lead a respectable life and you will be able to set a good example for your kids as well. You might even be able to leave something for the next generation. Earning money will not be enough if you are unable to preserve it. Your money-management skills will determine how your children will behave around money, which is why you have to ensure that you provide for everything and plan ahead of time.

WORKSHEET: AM I ON TRACK FOR RETIREMENT?

By the time you reach 30, experts recommend that you must have savings equal to your annual income. So if you are making $35,000 in a year, your savings must be $35,000. However, this might become a problem if your income is insufficient and you have many expenses to incur. As a starting point, you have to aim to save around 15% of your annual income at age 25 and 50% of your portfolio should consist of stocks. The general recommendations for retirement savings are as follows:

- Age 40: Twice your annual salary
- Age 50: Four times your annual salary
- Age 60: Six times your annual salary
- Age 67: Eight times your annual salary

Once you know these figures, fill out the following worksheet to know where you stand.

Questions	Your Comments Here
What is your age and annual salary?	
How many years do you have left till retirement?	
How much is your current savings?	
What does your portfolio look like?	
Compare your savings with the ideal figures given above. Is there a difference? If yes, how much are you falling short?	
What steps will you be taking to improve your savings goals?	

10

PAY IT FORWARD

It's not how much money you make, but how much money you keep, how hard it works for you, and how many generations you keep it for. –Robert Kiyosaki

My father had an intense passion for gardening. We did not have a huge house growing up, but our yard had the best garden in the entire neighborhood. Every Sunday my dad, my sister and I used to tend to the garden before lunch. Both my sister and I picked up on this habit because we associated gardening with family time and taking care of something other than ourselves. Children are like playdough—you can shape them any way you like. They will pick up most of their habits from their parents which is why it is very important to set a good example for them.

Financial literacy is the best gift that you can give your children. Every year millions of young adults enter the workplace with zero or very little knowledge about their finances. As parents, it is your responsibility to imbibe this financial wisdom in your children from a young age. The earlier you start, the better are their chances of developing a healthy relationship with money.

TEACHING YOUR CHILDREN ABOUT MONEY

Most parents make the mistake of thinking that children need to be older to know certain things. The truth is, most children find out about those so-called 'prohibited' things on their own and develop an unhealthy attitude about the same. Money is one topic most parents don't like to discuss with their children and as a result many children have absurd ideas about how money works. It is not cute for children to think that money grows on trees. Sure, money is something that they have to deal with as they grow up even if you don't teach them. However, if you teach them they will be able to handle it better and not face the common difficulties that many adults have to go through. Children develop most of their habits in their early years, which is why if you are not careful they might never truly learn to deal with their finances.

One summer many years ago, I had to share my room with my cousin who used to sneak out every night to meet her friends. One day I asked her where she went, to which she made a baby voice and told me she went downstairs to get some water. I was a child then but I knew that she was lying. Children are not easy to fool and they are more sensitive than you can imagine. If you tell them the truth and be honest with them, they will appreciate you more. Money is not like Santa Claus; you don't have to keep it a secret.

The first step in introducing your children to money would be to tell them what it is and how you get it. Don't give them the dictionary meaning, of course. Teach them that money is something that is earned and cannot be obtained just like that. Associate money with work so that they understand its value. Once they know the basics, you can slowly introduce them to cash and coins. My first physical interaction with money was when I was four or five years old, and my mother had asked me to pay a vendor at the park for my popsicle. I found money very intriguing and treated it as something quite precious as it gave me the gift of my favorite snack.

Tell your children how money works and let them build a positive relationship with money. They must understand the cycle that you need money to buy things and you need to work to earn money. You should always give your kids money as a reward, not as a bribe. The attitude should be "you did some good work, here is your reward" not "stop doing that and you will be rewarded." The former will encourage them to work hard while the latter will fuel negative intentions.

The other day I was at Target, waiting at the checkout counter behind a woman with her small daughter. The girl was around five years old and she kept demanding that her mother buy her a fairy-finder. Her mom patiently said "no" for a long time until finally, she told her daughter that she had not brought enough money to buy it. The daughter replied, "But Mommy, you will give them the card and they will give you anything you want. Why do you need the money?" She got a scolding after that and became quiet, but I understood something in that moment. When you teach today's kids about money, you have to give them a brief about how digital money works as well. They cannot be allowed to think that a credit card is a magical instrument that pays for everything.

Today's complex economic climate has made it difficult for parents to teach their children about money. However, this complexity is the very reason why you should take extra care to communicate financial wisdom to your children. It is difficult and it will take a lot of time, but you cannot and should not avoid it. Here are a few steps that will help you teach your kids about money.

Encourage a Habit of Savings

You might have developed a well-organized savings plan for you and your family, but your child is completely unaware of the process. They never see you saving money, but they always see you spending. You go to the store to buy groceries, you order an array of things online, and you pay for things in front of your children. It is natural for your kids to develop an association with spending rather than saving money. That is why you have to consciously encourage a habit of savings within your children. Do the traditional thing of buying them a piggy bank so that they can put any money they get in there. Selecting a glass jar is advisable because that would help them see their savings grow over time. A visual representation is very important because it stays with them longer. Teach them that savings is a good thing and not a sacrifice that they have to make.

With younger kids, you must target short-term goals first. For instance, if they want a certain toy that costs around $15, you can give them a target to save $10. If they save $10, then you will give them the remaining $5 to buy the toy. They will take a while to save that money which will teach them not to give in to instant gratification as we talked about in Chapter 1. When your child gets older, they will automatically start thinking about long-term goals. You can motivate them by playing a fun game. Motivate them to start saving inside their glass jar. Check the jar after a month to calculate how much they have saved. For example, if they have saved $10, you put another $10 into the jar to match their savings. This will motivate them to save more because they know whatever they save will double when Mommy or Daddy adds the same amount to the jar.

Create Opportunities to Earn Money

When you tell your child that they need to work to earn money, they might think that working is something that adults do and that they have no scope of earning money. You can create opportunities for your child to earn money by rewarding them with an allowance. This must be in exchange for running errands or any other housework that they do. Involving them in chores will make them more involved in the household while they learn about the value of money. They must feel like they have earned it so try to be serious with them when you pay them. Deduct money from their allowance in case they are not performing well enough and reward them with a little extra when they have done a good job.

When they are old enough to be in the workforce, make sure they get a part time job, even if it's just for a few hours a week or during the holidays. This will provide many opportunities to learn about money and start their journey of financial independence. It also means that they will learn to work within a team from people of all ages and backgrounds. You could also encourage their entrepreneurial spirit – whether it's from setting up a lemonade stall, car washing, dog walking or other tasks. Both can provide important lessons in financial literacy and what it really means to earn a dollar.

Help Them Out

Teaching your children about money is going to be one of the most difficult things that you will do. They are going to need a lot of help, which is why your patience is of pivotal importance. The basic rules of personal finance remain the same for your children as well: Teach them about the importance of preparing and sticking to a budget as well as about spending limits in comparison to their income and to define their 'wants' and 'needs'. When you give them an allowance, communicate to them that it is not okay to spend all of it. You can give them the example of a candy bar— when somebody gives them a big candy bar, they must not eat all of it and instead save some for later. Teaching them the basics of budgeting will enable them to make better financial decisions when they're older. Promote a giving mindset from when they are children; let them select a charity of their choice and teach them to donate a part of their money towards philanthropic efforts. This will help them grow a good habit.

When your children have grown up a bit, teach them the basics of investing. You don't have to get technical, just let them know how the system works. Many teenagers become interested in investments and stock markets and many of them end up studying finance because of the knowledge they gained from their parents.

Set a Good Example

Your children might not pick up your good habits, but they will pick up the bad ones. If you are a reckless spender, there is a high chance that your child will be too. Our parents are the first people whom we interact with and their habits have a deep impact on us. Your child looks up to you, you are their superhero, and anything you do, they will try to replicate. You need to model very good financial behavior so that you set a good example for them. If you have a habit of spending excessively when you go grocery shopping, even if your child doesn't accompany you to the store, they will notice how much you buy and how there's always a lot of extra stuff at home which nobody uses. It will normalize a habit of over-spending at the grocery store because they saw you do it. You have to ensure that you are not sending wrong signals like this and consciously project good financial behavior.

You can earn millions of dollars during your lifetime but it will all go to waste if your children do not have the proper financial sense to manage it. Your responsibility does not end with sending your children to good schools and colleges, you have to ensure that they are truly educated. Financial independence is a long journey. Make your children worthy of whatever wealth you have achieved so that they appreciate its value and can appreciate it in value.

Teach them to make good choices so that they can continue the good financial practices that you started. Trust yourself, and they will trust you. It all starts with you but make sure it doesn't end with you. True wealth is acquired over generations. Lead the way for a better and brighter tomorrow.

WORKSHEET: BRAINSTORM WAYS TO GET YOUR KIDS INCLUDED IN FINANCES

Based on the recommendations of this chapter, come up with three concrete ways that you can start teaching your kids about money.

What you wish to do: This will include any activity or lesson that you want to teach your child about in regards to money. List at least 3.	How do you plan on doing it? Will it be a regular activity or a one-time thing? Write your course of action.	Are there any possible challenges that may arise while doing the activity?	Follow up: After you have done the activity, how did your child react? Note the subsequent follow-ups and reactions as well and track how the reactions change over time.

AFTERWORD

When you bring a puppy home, she has no idea about how to behave. She chews on everything, often has bathroom accidents, and gets hyper for no reason. As she grows accustomed to you and your family, you teach her basic commands like 'sit' or 'stay.' You don't hurry or get impatient because you know it will be a while before she fully understands you. After a while, she will automatically be able to read your moods and snuggle up to you when you are upset.

Our minds are like that small puppy. It is resistant to all new things, especially if it involves stepping out of our comfort zone. Since most of us are used to having an unhealthy relationship with money, financial management seems like an uphill battle at first. However, you cannot give up and you need to be patient with yourself. Saving those first $1,000 is going to be your biggest challenge because your heart will keep tempting you to buy that lipstick or order takeout on a lazy Saturday. You might not see it at first, but every small temptation you fight will eventually add up and help you create wealth.

Building up a healthy financial mindset is the most important part of money management. You can be highly educated or even have a high-paying job, but without the right outlook, you won't be able to form good money habits. A healthy financial mindset will give you the motivation to prepare budgets and stick to them. It will facilitate debt management and remove the 'fear' of money. Once you get into these habits, you will start exploring other income opportunities and think about investing money to enhance your wealth. Your mindset will shift from "making ends meet" to "leading a financially stable life." Your life decisions will become more well-thought and you will easily be able to think about retirement because you will already be in the process of creating a provision for your old age. Homeownership won't seem as overwhelming as before if you know the logic behind making it work. Finally, you will be able to communicate this mentality to your children, thereby ensuring the safety of your financial legacy.

It might seem ironic coming from the author, but reading this book is not going to solve all your financial problems. I won't make you any false promises because you deserve my honesty. I am not here to teach you a class in finance but to help you navigate your way through common financial difficulties. Changes are only possible when you are willing to work for them because at the end of the day everything depends on your attitude.

You have already come a long way since the beginning of the book and you have more clarity about how to manage money. Now all you have to do is implement everything you have learned to seal the deal. Use the worksheets at the end of every chapter to record your opinions and track your progress in every aspect of money management. You can always modify the worksheets as per your needs. Make as many adjustments as you want, but don't give up on this journey once you have started. You have the potential to do great things and don't let anything or anybody convince you otherwise. You have the tools and you have the knowledge, now go out there and make a difference.

If you liked this book and it helped you solve some of your queries about money management, please leave a review. I would love to hear your feedback. Cheers!

REFERENCES

Alvarez, J. (2020 July 20). *Good debt vs. bad debt: why what you've been told is probably wrong*. CNBC. https://www.cnbc.com/2020/07/20/good-debt-vs-bad-debt-why-what-youve-been-told-is-probably-wrong.html

America Saves. (n.d.). *54 ways to save money*. https://americasaves.org/resource-center/insights/54-ways-to-save-money/

Anderson, L., & Taylor, A. (2016 September 19). *The Instagram effect: how the psychology of envy drives consumerism*. Deseret News. https://www.deseret.com/2016/9/19/20596477/the-instagram-effect-how-the-psychology-of-envy-drives-consumerism#posting-products-to-instagram-and-other-social-media-platforms-and-then-sharing-photos-online-is-changing-the-face-of-consumerism-in-america

Ashford, K. (2020 August 12). *What is compound interest?* Forbes Advisor. https://www.forbes.com/advisor/investing/compound-interest/

Bell, A. (2020 January 28). *6 Reasons why you NEED a budget.* Investopedia. https://www.investopedia.com/financial-edge/1109/6-reasons-why-you-need-a-budget.aspx

Berger, R. (2014 April 30). *Top 100 money quotes of all time.* Forbes. https://www.forbes.com/sites/robertberger/2014/04/30/top-100-money-quotes-of-all-time/?sh=7e7fe024998d

Board of Governors of the Federal Reserve System. (2018, May 22). *Federal Reserve Board issues report on the economic well-being of U.S. households.* https://www.federalreserve.gov/newsevents/pressreleases/other20180522a.htm

BrainyQuote. (n.d.). *936 Debt Quotes.* https://www.brainyquote.com/topics/debt-quotes

BrainyQuote. (n.d.). *Home ownership quotes.* https://www.brainyquote.com/topics/home-ownership-quotes

Buchenau, Z. (2019 November 7). *The importance of saving money: 15 reasons to start saving.* Be the Budget. https://bethebudget.com/the-importance-of-saving-money/

Burt, E. (2013 December 19). *Five steps to negotiating a raise. Kiplinger.* https://www.kiplinger.com/article/business/t012-c006-s001-five-steps-to-negotiating-a-raise.html

Caldwell, M. (2021 July 19). *5 Budget hacks to make your life easier.* The Balance. https://www.thebalance.com/budget-hacks-make-life-easier-2385611

Chappelow, J. (2019). *Gig economy.* Investopedia. https://www.investopedia.com/terms/g/gig-economy.asp

Chen, J. (2020 November 27). *Home equity.* Investopedia. https://www.investopedia.com/terms/h/home_equity.asp

CHEN, J. (2020). *Investment strategy.* Investopedia. https://www.investopedia.com/terms/i/investmentstrategy.asp

Cobra Financial Solutions Ltd. (2021, July 14). *How contactless payments can lead to bad debt.*https://cobrafinancial.co.uk/blog/how-contactless-payments-can-lead-to-bad-debt/

Consumer Financial Protection Bureau. (n.d.). *Use this debt worksheet to see all your bills and plan what you owe. https://files.consumerfinance.gov/f/documents/cfpb_well-being_debt-worksheet.pdf*

Cook, V., & Blacklock, A. (2019 October 31). *Financial fears: 17 common money worries.* Women Who Money. https://womenwhomoney.com/common-financial-fears-overcome-money-worries/

Cruze, R. (2021 August 26). *How to change your spending habits.* Ramsey Solutions. https://www.ramseysolutions.com/budgeting/money-habits-we-need-to-break

Daly, L. (2019 November 1). *Americans' 5 most common money worries.* The Motley Fool. https://www.fool.com/the-ascent/banks/articles/americans-5-most-common-money-worries/

Draper, S. (2019 December 16). *Council post: why financial literacy in schools matters today for the workforce of tomorrow.* Forbes. https://www.forbes.com/sites/forbescommunicationscouncil/2019/12/16/why-financial-literacy-in-schools-matters-today-for-the-workforce-of-tomorrow/?sh=3c60faf9110c

Egen, S. P. (2020). *10 Famous quotes about finances & credit.* Credit One Bank. https://www.creditonebank.com/articles/10-famous-quotes-about-finances-credit

Elkins, K. (2016a September 12). *Here's how much the average American family has saved for retirement.* CNBC. https://www.cnbc.com/2016/09/12/heres-how-much-the-average-american-family-has-saved-for-retirement.html

Elkins, K. (2016b October 3). *Here's how much Americans at every age have in their savings accounts.* CNBC. https://www.cnbc.com/2016/10/03/how-much-americans-at-every-age-have-in-their-savings-accounts.html

Elkins, K. (2017 April 26). *7 signs you're not saving enough money.* CNBC. https://www.cnbc.com/2017/04/26/signs-youre-not-saving-enough-money.html

Eneriz, A. (2021 April 28). *Debt avalanche vs. debt snowball: what's the difference?* Investopedia. https://www.investopedia.com/articles/personal-finance/080716/debt-avalanche-vs-debt-snowball-which-best-you.asp#debt-avalanche

Fay, B. (2012). *Good debt vs. bad debt - types of good and bad debts.* Debt.org. https://www.debt.org/advice/good-vs-bad/

Fay, B. (2019). *The U.S. consumer debt crisis.* Debt.org. https://www.debt.org/faqs/americans-in-debt/

Federal Trade Commission. (n.d.). *Make a budget.* https://www.consumer.ftc.gov/articles/pdf-1020-make-budget-worksheet.pdf

Fernando, J. (2019). *Compound interest definition.* Investopedia. https://www.investopedia.com/terms/c/compoundinterest.asp

Fontinelle, A. (2019). *9 Reasons to say no to credit.* Investopedia. https://www.investopedia.com/articles/younginvestors/08/purchase-financing.asp

Fontinelle, A. (2021, August 31). *7 smart steps every new homeowner should take. Investopedia.* https://www.investopedia.com/articles/mortgages-real-estate/09/new-homeowner-tips.asp

Ganti, A. (2019). *Asset class definition.* Investopedia. https://www.investopedia.com/terms/a/assetclasses.asp

Google Sheets. (n.d.). *Debt snowball spreadsheet.* https://docs.google.com/spreadsheets/d/1duZTwQMeNt6xqFIQ_g0QT3b0hfzNms4rUUZSL9TLvcY/template/preview

Hayes, A. (2020 November 27). *After-tax real rate of return.* Investopedia. https://www.investopedia.com/terms/a/after-tax-real-rate-of-return.asp

Huddleston, C. (2020 February 13). *How to teach your kids good money habits.* Forbes Advisor. https://www.forbes.com/advisor/personal-finance/how-to-teach-your-kids-good-money-habits/

Hughes, N. (2017 July 21). *Credit cards: the psychology behind the plastic.* Baker Tilly. https://www.bakertilly.ie/credit-cards-psychology-behind-plastic/

Indeed Editorial Team. (2021 February 23). *How to negotiate a raise in 7 steps.* https://www.indeed.com/career-advice/pay-salary/how-to-negotiate-raise

Indeed. (2021). *Salesperson salary in United States.*https://www.indeed.com/career/salesperson/salaries

Internationalinsurance.com. (2016). *How much does healthcare cost in the USA?* https://www.internationalinsurance.com/resources/healthcare-costs-in-the-usa.php

Jayakumar, A. (2021 February 10). *What is debt consolidation, and should I consolidate?* NerdWallet. https://www.nerdwallet.com/article/finance/consolidate-debt

Jespersen, C. (2020 May 13). *How to save money: 17 tips.* NerdWallet. https://www.nerdwallet.com/article/finance/how-to-save-money

Johnson, H. (2021 May 10). *The best coupon apps for 2021.* Investopedia. https://www.investopedia.com/best-coupon-apps-5181187

Kagan, J. (2019). *Credit score.* Investopedia. https://www.investopedia.com/terms/c/credit_score.asp

Kagan, J. (2020 December 28). *Debt consolidation.* Investopedia. https://www.investopedia.com/terms/d/debtconsolidation.asp

Kahneman, D., & Deaton, A. (2010). *High income improves evaluation of life but not emotional well-being.* Proceedings of the National Academy of Sciences, 107(38), 16489–16493. https://doi.org/10.1073/pnas.1011492107

Kemenes, P. (2021 May 5). *Is Afterpay safe?* Wise. https://wise.com/us/blog/is-afterpay-safe

Kerr, A. (2019). *Financial Independence, Retire Early (FIRE).* Investopedia. https://www.investopedia.com/terms/f/financial-independence-retire-early-fire.asp

Klimashousky, D. (2019 July 23). *Making an investment plan: a step-by-step guide.* SmartAsset. https://smartasset.com/investing/how-to-make-an-investment-plan

Kushi, O. (2020 November 5). *Homeownership remains strongly linked to wealth-building.* First American. https://blog.firstam.com/economics/homeownership-remains-strongly-linked-to-wealth-building

Lake, R. (2021 November 14). *What is buy now, pay later?* Investopedia. https://www.investopedia.com/buy-now-pay-later-5182291

Lee, E. (2014 December 2). *Will Apple Pay sabotage your spending budget?* CNBC. https://www.cnbc.com/2014/12/02/will-apple-pay-sabotage-your-spending-budget.html

Lee, J., & Pyles, S. (2020 May 28). *How to get out of debt: 7 tips that work.* NerdWallet. https://www.nerdwallet.com/article/finance/tips-for-paying-off-debt-from-people-who-did-it

Majaski, C. (2019). *The difference between renting and owning a home.* Investopedia. https://www.investopedia.com/articles/personal-finance/083115/renting-vs-owning-home-pros-and-cons.asp

Marquit, M. (2020 June 15). *Retirement basics: what is a 401(k) plan?* Forbes Advisor. https://www.forbes.com/advisor/retirement/what-is-401k/

Martin, E. (2018a March 15). *65% of Americans save little or nothing—and half could end up struggling in retirement.* CNBC. https://www.cnbc.com/2018/03/15/bankrate-65-percent-of-americans-save-little-or-nothing.html

Martin, E. (2018b June 25). *Only 47% of Americans have enough emergency savings—but most people aren't worried.* CNBC. https://www.cnbc.com/2018/06/22/how-much-money-you-should-put-in-your-emergency-fund.html

Money Habitudes. (2012, April 4). *Spending habits: understanding and changing.* https://www.moneyhabitudes.com/blog/understanding-spending-habits/

Money Management International. (n.d.). *Ultimate guide to creating a budget.* https://www.moneymanagement.org/budget-guides/create-a-budget

Mozo. (2021 June 7). *Love afterpay? Here are the traps you should know about.* https://mozo.com.au/fintech/love-afterpay-here-are-the-traps-you-should-know-about

Murphy, C. B. (2019). *How lenders and banks use your debt-to-income ratio – DTI.* Investopedia. https://www.investopedia.com/terms/d/dti.asp

Napoletano, E. (2020 July 28). *What is investing? How can you start investing?* Forbes Advisor. https://www.forbes.com/advisor/investing/what-is-investing/

NerdWallet. (2020 September 4). *What's the difference between a soft inquiry and a hard inquiry on my credit report?* https://www.nerdwallet. com/article/finance/credit-report-soft-hard-pull-difference

NerdWallet. (2021 July 7). *Debt-to-income ratio: how to calculate your DTI.* https://www.nerdwallet.com/article/loans/personal-loans/ calculate-debt-income-ratio

O'Shea, A. (2021 August 18). *Different types of stocks you should know.* NerdWallet. https://www.nerdwallet.com/article/investing/types-of-stocks

O'Shea, B. (2021 October 13). *Does debt consolidation hurt your credit?* NerdWallet. https://www.nerdwallet.com/article/finance/does-debt-consolidation-hurt-credit

O'Shea, B., & Pyles, S. (2021a April 23). *How to use debt avalanche.* NerdWallet. https://www.nerdwallet.com/article/finance/what-is-a-debt-avalanche

O'Shea, B., & Pyles, S. (2021b April 23). *How to use debt snowball to pay off debt.* NerdWallet. https://www.nerdwallet.com/article/ finance/what-is-a-debt-snowball?trk_channel=web&trk_copy= How%20to%20Use%20Debt%20Snowball%20to%20Pay%20Off% 20Debt&trk_element=hyperlink&trk_elementPosition=2& trk_location=PostList&trk_subLocation=next-steps

O'Shea, B., & Schwahn, L. (2021 January 13). *Budgeting 101: how to budget money.* NerdWallet. https://www.nerdwallet.com/article/ finance/how-to-budget

Orem, T. (2021 July 28). *Complete guide to retirement planning: everything you need to know.* NerdWallet. https://www.nerdwallet.com/article/investing/retirement-planning-an-introduction

Pant, P. (2020 November 28). *How to prioritize your budget with 5 simple categories.* The Balance. https://www.thebalance.com/how-to-prioritize-your-budget-453693

Pant, P. (2021 July 15). *The perfect budget worksheet to manage your savings goals.* The Balance. https://www.thebalance.com/budget-worksheet-savings-goals-453595

Patel, N. (2014). *The psychology of instant gratification and how it will revolutionize your marketing approach.* Entrepreneur. https://www.entrepreneur.com/article/235088

Kagan, J. (2020 September 29). *5 key retirement-planning steps everyone should take.* Investopedia. https://www.investopedia.com/articles/retirement/11/5-steps-to-retirement-plan.asp

Probasco, J. (2019). *All the pros and cons of investing in a home.* Investopedia. https://www.investopedia.com/articles/mortgages-real-estate/08/home-ownership.asp

Probasco, J. (2020). *How much do I need to retire?* Investopedia. https://www.investopedia.com/retirement/how-much-you-should-have-saved-age/

Psychology Today. (2019). *Habit Formation.* https://www.psychologytoday.com/us/basics/habit-formation

R.L. Adams. (2017 June 19). *50 ideas for a lucrative side hustle.* Entrepreneur. https://www.entrepreneur.com/article/293954

Ramsey Solutions. (2021a September 27). *15 ways to teach kids about money*. Ramsey Solutions. https://www.ramseysolutions.com/ relationships/how-to-teach-kids-about-money

Ramsey Solutions. (2021b November 5). *What Is the F.I.R.E. Movement?* https://www.ramseysolutions.com/retirement/what-is-the-fire-movement

Regions. (2019). *10 best ways to save money*. https://www.regions. com/Insights/Personal/Personal-Finances/budgeting-and-saving/ 10-Best-Ways-to-Save-Money

Rose, S. (2021 March 18). *Savings worksheet to crush your money goals*. OppLoans. https://www.opploans.com/oppu/articles/savings-worksheet/

Sallie Mae Bank. (n.d.). *My monthly budget worksheet*. https://www. salliemae.com/content/dam/slm/legacy/assets/college-planning/ monthly-budget-worksheet.pdf

Schwab Moneywise. (n.d.). *Investor profile questionnaire*. https:// www.schwabmoneywise.com/resource/smw-investor-profile-questionnaire

Sinicki, A. (2021 May 21). Upwork vs Fiverr: *Which is the best place to sell your services?* Android Authority. https://www. androidauthority.com/upwork-vs-fiverr-1190439/

Smith, K. A. (2019 August 2). *The Forbes guide to individual retirement accounts (IRAs)*. Forbes Advisor. https://www.forbes.com/advisor/ retirement/the-forbes-guide-to-individual-retirement-accounts-iras/

Smith, L. (2019). *Good debt vs. bad debt: What's the difference?* Investopedia. https://www.investopedia.com/articles/pf/12/good-debt-bad-debt.asp

SoFi. (2021, June 3). *The 50/30/20 Rule Demystified.* https://www.sofi.com/learn/content/50-30-20-budget/?__cf_chl_jschl_tk__=9GmOdAYbuDds3OQIEOV.vTKjhWgnuTGFyU4zjTbhsbY-1637386519-0-gaNycGzNCH0

Solis, B. (2017 November 20). *Impatience is a virtue: how the on-demand economy is making mobile consumers impatient.* Forbes. https://www.forbes.com/sites/briansolis/2017/11/20/impatience-is-a-virtue-how-the-on-demand-economy-is-making-mobile-consumers-impatient/?sh=29022a37344c

Staff, S. (2019 May 30). *10 meaningful quotes about achieving financial freedom.* SUCCESS. https://www.success.com/10-meaningful-quotes-about-achieving-financial-freedom/

Stieg, C. (2020 May 26). *From the "perfect" salary to keeping up with the Joneses, here's how money really affects your happiness.* CNBC. https://www.cnbc.com/2020/05/26/how-your-salary-and-the-way-you-spend-money-affect-your-happiness.html

Tan, W. (2021 August 10). *The "buy now, pay later" trend could be the next hidden source of consumer debt, analysts warn.* CNBC. https://www.cnbc.com/2021/08/10/buy-now-pay-later-instalment-plans-may-cause-consumer-credit-card-debt-to-rise.html

The Wealthfront Team. (2019 June 5). *Is it better to rent or buy a home? How to decide which is best for you.* Wealthfront Blog. https://blog.wealthfront.com/renting-vs-buying-a-home/

Time Rowe Price Insights. (n.d.). *Are My Retirement Savings on Track?* https://www.troweprice.com/content/dam/iinvestor/resources/insights/pdfs/whats-my-savings-benchmark-are-my-retirement-savings-on-track.pdf

Turbo. (2018 October 15). *60 super simple ways to save money.* Mint-Life Blog. https://mint.intuit.com/blog/real-money-talk/how-to-save-money-1358/

Univest. (n.d.). *Pros & cons of buying a house.* Www.univest.net. https://www.univest.net/personal-banking/renting-vs-buying

Vohwinkle, J. (2019). *Your 6-step guide to making a personal budget.* The Balance. https://www.thebalance.com/how-to-make-a-budget-1289587

Voigt, K., & Benson, A. (2021 November 22). *What is a bond: definition and facts.* NerdWallet. https://www.nerdwallet.com/article/investing/what-is-a-bond

Voigt, K., & O'Shea, A. (2021 March 17). *Definition: what is stock?* NerdWallet. https://www.nerdwallet.com/article/investing/what-is-a-stock

Want to teach your kids about money? *Preach these 3 principles.* (n.d.). NBC News. https://www.nbcnews.com/better/lifestyle/how-teach-young-kids-about-money-so-it-sticks-them-ncna1023231

Williams, G. (2021 May 17). *Renting vs. buying a home: which is smarter?* US News. https://realestate.usnews.com/real-estate/articles/renting-vs-buying-a-home-which-is-smarter

REFERENCES

Winderl, A. M. (2020 April 6). *Why forming good money habits is important for financial success.* Earnest. https://www.earnest.com/blog/good-money-habits/

Zimmermann, J. (2019 June 29). *Side hustles you can start with no money.* NerdWallet. https://www.nerdwallet.com/article/small-business/side-hustles-can-start-no-money

ABOUT THE AUTHOR

Morgan Johns is a financial educator and the author of *How to Manage Your Money Like an Adult in 7 Easy Steps*.

Morgan's rich career history involves work in personal banking, mortgage advice, portfolio management, and property coaching. Skilled at helping clients with budget management and realistic, result-driven wealth creation. Morgan believes that it's not enough to simply tell clients how to manage their budgets, and has an ethos of showing them where they're going wrong and drawing attention to their unconscious spending habits. Morgan is passionate about financial literacy and education and believes that everyone has it within their power to take control of their finances.

Morgan's passion for helping others get ahead stems from a working class background and a determination to better her own financial reality. The results were astounding, and this sparked a passion for financial education. Morgan has been investing in property for over 20 years and is proud to have a healthy share portfolio and a sizable property portfolio. Throughout her career, she became increasingly aware of the gender gap when it comes to finances and is passionate about getting women engaged in their finances.

Morgan's main passion in life is helping other people navigate their finances, but also recognizes the value of taking a breath to enjoy the beauty in life. Morgan loves being outside in nature and can often be found walking, running, or cycling around local beauty spots.

Made in the USA
Columbia, SC
21 April 2023

15679100R00085